SHIVA SPEAKS

Books by Rashmi Khilnani

The Divine Mother Speaks: The Healing of the Human Heart

Buddha Speaks: To the Buddha Nature Within

SHIVA SPEAKS

Conversations *with*
Maha Avatar Babaji

RASHMI KHILNANI

RAINBOW RIDGE
BOOKS

Cover and Interior design by Frame25 Productions
Cover photographs © Mayboroda and iulias c/o Shutterstock.com

Published by:
Rainbow Ridge Books, LLC
140 Rainbow Ridge Road
Faber, Virginia 22938
434-361-1723

If you are unable to order this book from your local
bookseller, you may order directly from the distributor.

Square One Publishers, Inc.
115 Herricks Road
Garden City Park, NY 11040
Phone: (516) 535-2010
Fax: (516) 535-2014
Toll-free: 877-900-BOOK

Visit the author at:
www.reiki-energy-mastery.com

Library of Congress Cataloging-in-Publication Data applied for.

ISBN 978-1-937907-14-3

10 9 8 7 6 5 4 3 2 1

Printed on acid-free paper in the United States

He encompasses all things,
Though He is but One.
Whoever should know him,
Shiva the Benign,
wins peace forever.

—Svetashvatara Upanishad, 1V:14

I dedicate this book to beloved Babaji and my noble friend St Enoch of St Albans.

CONTENTS

Dedication   vii

PART I: Maha Avatar Babaji

Chapter One
Babaji, the Guru of Gurus   3

Chapter Two
My Spiritual Journey with Babaji   9

Chapter Three
The Coming Age of Light   25

PART II: Maha Avatar Babaji Teaches Us Here Now

Introduction   37

Chapter Four
Love Is   41

Chapter Five
Courage   51

Chapter Six
I Am Harmony   59

Chapter Seven
Om Namah Shivaya   63

Chapter Eight
Humor   67

Chapter Nine
Intuition and Doubt   71

Chapter Ten
Accelerated Transformation   75

Chapter Eleven
Faith and Trust   81

Chapter Twelve
Truth   87

Chapter Thirteen
Simplicity   91

Chapter Fourteen
Bridging of the Spiritual and the Mundane   95

Chapter Fifteen
Dare to Be Your Truth   103

Chapter Sixteen
Grace and Purity of Heart   113

Chapter Seventeen
Rashmi's Conclusion   119

Acknowledgments   121

Biography of Rashmi Khilnani   123

PART ONE

MAHA AVATAR BABAJI

Chapter One

BABAJI, THE GURU OF GURUS

YES! THE SAME BABAJI from Yogananda's *An Autobiography of a Yogi!* Yet, how do you define the indefinable limitless incarnation of divine energy in a human body?

It is impossible! An experiential glimpse into the vast benediction and grace of this magnificent force field of Shiva Beingness comes suddenly and out of the blue, and all because of one's deep heartfelt longing, prayer, or devotion. For many, seeing a picture of Bhole Baba awakens the supreme unlimited vastness of the soul and its incomprehensible connection with the Oversoul.

Babaji taught Jesus, Moses, Elijah and many, many other saints, gurus and people who have walked the earth walk. As an Ascended Master, he is the Christ Yogi who is with us on Planet Earth—sometimes in a body or several, and sometimes as an etheric presence and usually as both. He will remain with us until seven billion plus humans achieve "Christ Consciousness," or call it "Enlightenment," or the "moving out of the consciousness of linear time and space into the Eternal Now."

He is my best friend, my Guru of Gurus, my "24-hour come-dian." He makes me laugh and laugh and laugh. His teachings are simple and powerful. Encapsulated in three words: truth, love, and simplicity. In this time of colossal, political, economic, ecological, social, and psychological change, He is here to help us, to guide us, to coax us, and to inspire humanity to move gracefully into the energies of the Age of Aquarius—an age of light after a period of 13,000 years of slumber and darkness.

As the Bible says, "Ask and you shall receive." His celestial gifts are more easily available through his recommended spiritual prac-tice of *Jappa* (repeating the name of Shiva or any other name of the divine), *Karma Yoga* (the path of conscious work), *Puja* (ceremonial devotion to the divine), and celebrating through song and dance the holy names of God/Goddess in His/Her myriad forms.

On my path, I have met an interesting assortment of enlight-ened beings; but, through being reconnected to Babaji fifteen years ago in this lifetime, he has become "My All and Everything." Why not go to the main source—the supreme cosmic energy station—directly?

As a teacher of Reiki Masters into the many streams of Reiki wisdom teachings of Universal life-force energy, one works with and channels the energies of many beautiful divine beings such as Quan Yin, Buddha, Avalokitesvara, and Jesus. Babaji shines forth as my Supreme Master. I speak to him on a daily basis, and I have asked to serve the divine plan as best as I can, to follow my intuition moment to moment, and so Babaji gives me places to go, people to meet, and energies to shift across the globe (within free will and the highest good of all).

All this might sound like a lot of hard work, but the truth is that Haidakhan Baba is funny, quick-witted, and can be as mischie-vous as a monkey at times (the energy of Hanuman) in the way he teaches, guides, and illuminates the tempestuous, courageous, and crazy path of self-realization. This is not an easy spiritual road for those who are half-hearted about discovering who they are. It is like walking on the razor's edge on the one hand, and an incredible fun-filled adventure on the other. If you don't want to be shifted out of your little box of reality, then reading this book and connecting to Lord Shiva can be a challenge for you.

People the world over comment that I live a life of freedom, like a "celeb" minus the paparazzi, and they wish to join the party! Such a life of spontaneity, adventure, and liberty is available to all of humanity as they let go of limitation and control.

If, however, you wish to choose to pursue money for money's sake, lust over love, and a lack of integrity in the name of quick profit, then as a pristine manifester of your own reality, that is what you are going to get. For me, the challenge is keeping one part of me firmly grounded as a human while the other part is happy being a spiritual space cadet—finding divine balance being the key.

On the other hand, I trust completely in the divine with Babaji, as a name for "All That Is," guiding me moment to moment to make the right choices, fun choices, and choices that lead to the highest good of all concerned in each scenario. In fact I see and feel Babaji and my Higher Self as synonymous.

I invite you on this journey, through sharing of my experiences with Babaji and my spiritual path, and to a dance of celebration, ecstasy, and bliss, and to hearing his sacred teachings. I invite you to embrace an unimaginable freedom and to become more and more fearless—not by avoiding fear but by going through it and coming out the other side.

I have always felt like a spiritual princess and been called one wherever I go. Some people feel that you cannot be spiritual and abundant at the same time. This is one of the greatest mistakes that many humans make on their life journeys. As Jesus said, "It is the *Kingdom* of Heaven." Ultimately the crucial thing to remember is

not how much or how little we have, but how much we allow ourselves to feel in the cosmic flow and share of that flow even if it is in
the richness of a smile.

Connecting to Babaji is, as I have said before, like connecting to the "cosmic plug" and switching it on. Shiva is all-pervasive,
all-knowing, multidimensional being and becoming. Babaji is *Sada
Shiva* (*sada* means eternal). In the early 1970s, he manifested miraculously in the body of a 18-year-old youth in a cave in Haidakhan (a
tiny village in the Himalayan foothills) where he has been appearing
in different bodies many times over many centuries.

Shri Maha Avatar Babaji has given *Kriya Yoga* to the planet
and rebirthing through one of his favorite devotees, Leonard Orr.
He has also impulsed many other amazing modalities of healing for
mankind. He gives his blessings to all denominations and respects
all pathways to the divine.

Babaji is "*Satyam Shivam Sundaram.*" These Sanskrit words mean
Satyam: Supreme Truth; *Shivam*: Infinite Supreme Consciousness;
Sundaram: Supreme Beauty. (I think you will agree with me from
pictures of Babaji in his 1970s incarnation that he is extremely good
looking!)

Babaji's compassion and the way he teaches constantly amaze,
fascinate, and stupefy me. No matter how clever I think I am, he
is usually six steps ahead and he knows that in my case, the best
way to get me into a spiritual click is to make me see the hysteri-
cal aspect of so-called "reality" and the cosmic joke behind most
dramas.

I would like to clarify that this ecstatic path is not free of all the
usual human conundrums and intense challenges of the times. It is
not like I don't feel frustration or anger, and it is not as though my
relationships are always perfect. However, thanks to Babaji's grace,
which comes from my aligning my higher will with his divine will,
a magic cloak of calm, peace, and joy pervade my being no matter

how much I am otherwise kicking and screaming on the personality level.

Babaji says that this a time of *"Maha Kranti,"* or the great purging of Mother Earth and her peoples. Thus, he highly recommends the regular chanting of the *Maha Mantra "Om Namah Shivaya,"* which means: I love myself, I honor myself, and the God/Goddess dwells within me as me. Come on everyone; let's join in the Shiva Party!

OM NAMAH SHIVAYA

This *"Om Namah Shivaya"* was written and drawn in Babaji's own handwriting as Haidakhan Babaji in the 1970s.

Chapter Two

MY SPIRITUAL JOURNEY WITH BABAJI

MY CONNECTION TO THE divine goes back to my conception in Egypt, very close to the Great Pyramids of Giza. I have recall in trance states of my soul's journey coming down from Source to the higher realms of Venus and this energy stepping down to resonate with the blue-green light and love and sound of Mother Earth. But in spite of all this exalted understanding from childhood, paradoxically I have always struggled with the over-intellectual, highly analytical and, I hate to admit it, at times judgmental mind of mine.

In fact, in 2009 I had an amazing spiritual journey in India where I went to the banks of the River Jamuna, in Old Delhi, to witness the burning of the body of one who has passed over. I got to see in open-eyed meditation how the body goes back to the five elements—it literally dissolves back into earth, water, fire, and air and into ether. I was also blessed by being shown how the soul lifted out of the body as light into the burning flames of the funeral pyre and then took its ecstatic flight toward the greater light, the sun, and beyond.

This initiation—of facing my fear of death and of seeing beyond the veils—is one that I am integrating powerfully on many levels. What I have noticed is that my mind continues to ramble on and I feel a lot of fear sometimes, especially at night. I feel as though it is unspecific morphogenic fear and fear at the cellular memory levels. However, I manage now to feel more and more detached at the core and have a true experiential feeling that I am peace, I am calm, I am immortal being here now, in spite of the whirling thoughts, emotions, desires, and fears at the periphery.

One morning as I walked briskly to my friend Amravati's flat (during the period when I was channeling this book), I was talking to Babaji about how fed up I was with all this fear and intellectualization. He said to me simply, "You are the Sakshi, the detached witness of your body, mind, and intellect. Therefore, overidentification with thoughts, and any other negativity, gives these undesirable energies more power within your being. Just watch and let go of your attachment, for while you are in a body, the mind will think and fear and doubt. Remember, you are not the mind."

Working on this book, I have been asking myself and Babaji: what is the use of writing another spiritual book while humanity is reeling, especially in the Western Hemisphere—in debt, depletion, and various states of delusion while the bookshelves in bookstores are full of powerful gems of wisdom? Babaji has informed me that it is okay for me to feel world-weary from time to time. However, each new story of sharing from the heart can work exponentially to inspire, lift, and transform consciousness.

I have spent years and years on my spiritual path and in fact, lifetimes over eons of time. This may sound arrogant, but I can humbly say that I know I have achieved enlightenment in some of these lifetimes. But this is Rashmi, here now on planet Earth, obsessed with becoming enlightened, shifting and raising consciousness within and without, earnestly questioning "who am I?" and asking for the grace to see beyond the veils of 3D reality as a regular normal part of my awareness.

The point is that the wise aspect of my being understands totally—and something that I actually teach my students and other spiritual aspirants—that, ultimately, the paradox of my being is that there is no one here; there is no one aspiring, and the question to ask is: "Is there actually anyone thinking, feeling, fretting, etc.?"

Let me give you an example of this paradox: a while back, I went for a massage in St Albans and met a Reiki Master who worked on me. As she shared, I felt the experiential understanding that ultimately though I was receiving and also giving healing and instruction, that actually neither she nor I was doing anything.

The most important thing that I can ever practice on my path, and the most important teaching that I can impart to my students, is that of non-doership. To let go of the "I am doing," "I am feeling," and so on. This identification and preoccupation of the "I," or "the ego" is the root cause of all my suffering, and I note the suffering of all who come to me for healing.

Babaji constantly gives me an experiential understanding that I am at the "Heart of all Hearts." I am the "Soul of all Souls," and all of humanity is similarly part of One Supreme Consciousness, One Supreme Energy, which can be called: "All That Is," or call it unity consciousness, or Christ awareness, as you wish.

This is absolute reality and higher consciousness—expanded awareness. It is about coming out of limitation and control to the understanding and the moment-to-moment practice of keeping one's consciousness in the Absolute. The periphery of one's consciousness, i.e., the personality self, in the meanwhile can happily dance at the same time in relative states wherever the I—the ego—becomes relevant.

Babaji states that a true spiritual master is one that has embodied a moment-to-moment experiential balance of awareness between "The Supreme Unity of All That Is," at the center of one's being, and the relative state.

I would like to share with you that, every time I re-remind myself of the above wisdom, my life becomes easy, joyful, effortless—it becomes pure magic. These are times when I come out of fear, but when I act out of my ego, my mind becomes sticky and filled with the energy of struggle, worry, frustration, or stress.

It is so simple and yet I forget sometimes. The trick is not to be judgmental when that happens but just to forgive myself, pick myself out of the mud of false identification, and come back to the supreme calm of the inner silence of the Higher Self within me, where nothing is happening. It is very restful; I promise you.

How do you reach the state where you can accept that you are the detached witness of all That Is? For me, one of the greatest keys for self-realization has been Ramana Maharshi's "Who am I?" mediation and the reading of all his amazing books. Just looking at a picture of this beautiful being can take you into an instantaneous flight of meditative ecstasy.

In Haidakhan (Babaji's ashram in the Himalayan foothills), which to me feels like my spiritual home, chanting with Babaji and my fellow-devotees accelerates coming into this state where the "I" dissolves, and everything becomes One Energy and stillness at the same time. You can become it through dancing wholeheartedly, singing from your center, painting and running, etc. The key here is to become at one with and wholehearted about whichever path or activity you choose.

The practice of *Yagya*, or the ancient Vedantic Fire Ceremony with mantra and praise to the Divine Mother, with the fire as symbolic of the Mouth of the Goddess, is another amazing vehicle for me to instantly come into the grace of the state of Zen. For Leonard

Orr, the great spiritual purification enthusiast and father of rebirthing, sitting with fire and becoming at-one with it takes him into that state where his ego-self dissolves and he becomes "at-one-ment" and peace.

This brings us to Babaji's teaching of love. The heart is the hub of love. From the heart, love can emanate into the body, mind and spirit. Love unifies, love builds bridges, love chooses the highest good, and most of all love is about win-win scenarios. Love is not about competition and love is not about ego and love is not even about effort.

Love does not judge, it does not divide, and it does not try to dominate or rule. Babaji is all love. My sister and many others have often remarked that I am in a state of grace, and my mother says that I have a golden heart. I believe that all humanity is in a state of grace, which has been bestowed on us by the Goddess with gold-compassionate heart energy.

My heart has gotten me into a lot of trouble in my life. I have made some illogical choices, jumped off a few cliffs, caused myself much heartache, and many times it has led me to walk away on my journey. (I am not referring to romantic heart issues and expectations, or the psychology of the heart either.) The Golden Heart within each being is a very deep place within the entity, a place that is connected strongly to the Soul and the Oversoul. Being with Babaji will take you to that space within yourself, within an instant.

All you have to do is to intend it, become still and ask Babaji for his grace and help. On my spiritual journey, after recovery from second-grade invasive cancer, I asked Babaji to connect me to someone on the planet who loved him like I did and served Babaji like I intended and practiced.

Up popped Leonard Orr. We spent hours discussing our different meetings with Babaji and the various bodies with which He presented himself to us across the globe. Anyone overhearing our conversation would have thought we were seriously off the wall.

It is difficult to say when my spiritual journey began. Unlike a lot of new agers, I firmly believe that every aspect of my life is ultimately spiritual. This includes what many popularly describe as my "shadow self." As far as I am concerned, the shadow helps to define the light. My darkness has been a great teacher, instigator, and facilitator in pushing me onward into deeper and deeper self-discovery, knowledge, and a quest for experiential understanding on the path.

From pretty early on, I have had no patience or interest in knowledge for knowledge's sake. As a student and teacher of metaphysics, my bottom line has been an experiential comprehension and application of spiritual principles and impeccability of walking "one's talk" on the path. What has impressed and attracted me to various gurus and fellow aspirants is not how many qualifications they have or titles, or even how many people they have as part of their entourages. I have been more interested with how open is a person's heart and are they speaking their truth moment to moment as best as they can. The practice of wisdom and compassion and the balance between the practical and grounded, and at the same time being able to access expanded states of consciousness, is what interests me.

During my life, I have learned that the most amazing beings are oftentimes not found on the spiritual stage or in so-called spiritual centers, but are just normal simple people that pop up in sometimes the most unlikely of places. For instance, during my cancer treatment at the Royal Marsden Hospital in London, I was amazed at the dedication, healing energy, and sincerity of the doctors, nurses, and attendants in an allopathic center.

What I really loved was how much they honored me for being a holistic teacher of energy medicine and how open they were to the concept that prayer, love, and meditation can heal even more powerfully than mainstream medicine. As my surgeon very sweetly reminded me, at one of my visits to her at the time, *The Lancet*—one the world's leading medical journals—had reported the positive results of the power of prayer.

I wish that I will soon see this level of openness and tolerance amongst those on different spiritual paths and the honoring of other diverse denominations that may be contrary to their own chosen way.

Here we are in 2013 on Planet Earth, and I ask myself what has been my shadow lessons for half a century? My biggest lesson, and the darkest part of my being, has been impatience—what some even consider an asset. The tricky thing about the shadow is that very often one isn't even aware that it is triggering undesirable thoughts, emotions, and behavior.

Of course, there have been many other aspects linked to this core issue of wanting everything to happen the day before yesterday! If things don't happen fast enough, Rashmi could be prone to being angry, frustrated, irritated, and unnecessarily stressed out. The other part of darkness I have had to grapple with is twofold: boredom and fear that come from having an overly vivid imagination. To add to the long sorry list is the feeling at times of isolation and separation and wanting heaven on earth at all times.

My spiritual journey has helped me greatly with the above issues. As you know healing happens like peeling the layers of an onion and sometimes, if we work for years on the different layers of the issue, we come to the center of the onion, i.e., to nothingness.

Meditation, prayer, initiation into the many streams of Reiki Mastery, and meetings (Darshan) with enlightened beings has helped me greatly to come out of the dark night of the soul and into the light. Reading high-frequency channeled material and the ancient books of wisdom of many denominations has also helped me in coming out of the uncontrollable oscillation between the polarities (fear/love, heat/cold, stress/relaxation) to my center where all is still and calm and I am at one with the universe.

Years ago I found myself leaving a man I loved very much because he couldn't understand that the spiritual journey was very important to me, and he erroneously presumed that I loved God more than him. For me, *God and all I encounter are one*. At the time I had become a Karuna Reiki Master and had flown to India and found that my father's best friend, in spite of being a rich businessman, had forged signatures and sold my real estate shares and stolen my money. I was very focused on receiving the divine grace of Sai Baba and going to Shirdi as well, but as usual the divine came to my rescue, helped me retrieve the stolen money and complete the two holy pilgrimages as well. I flew back to London feeling very blessed but knowing that there was more to learn and more to discover of the great mystery.

At the home of a soul sister in Stroud, which was full of pictures of gurus and divine beings, I found myself mesmerized by a tiny picture in the kitchen of Maha Avatar Babaji. I was there for a Christmas party and found that I could not move away, for hours, from his presence.

Back in London, I was having endless philosophical chats with my friend and teacher Michael and found myself asking him what the next steps to enlightenment were. After being awkward and difficult for ages, he said, as we watched the children playing in the sand pit in Holland Park, "Rashmi, you are now a psychic surgeon, healer, and teacher. Maybe to round things off nicely, you can connect to rebirthing, Babaji, *Kriya Yoga*, and Jasmuheen's book *Living on Light*.

I didn't even have a piece of paper to write it all down. I panicked and felt overwhelmed and I couldn't understand the connection of all those different paths to the divine.

However, miraculously I found a wonderful rebirther named Gerd who, as per my usual synergy, turned out to also be the organizer for *Kriya Yoga* and Jasmuheen's workshops on "Living on Light" for London. During my rebirthing sessions, Gerd always had a big picture of his beloved Babaji within view of us. I was next initiated into *Kriya Yoga* and discovered that Babaji was the instigator and inspiration behind rebirthing, which is consciously connected breathing, *Kriya Yoga*. And the first chapter in Jasmuheen's book is all about Babaji.

I wanted a picture of this great being. I wanted to find out where I could perform divine ceremony to him, where I could chant his name, and find others who felt as strongly connected to this incredible emanation of the Divine Father/Mother energies.

Years earlier, when I lived in Dubai with my millionaire businessman husband, I had a vision of being in a coffin, leaving the kingdom of my homes across the globe, and of Lord Shiva asking me to let go of everything and to follow him as he swam under water in Lake Mansarovar in Tibet. In the vision I did not hesitate. I followed his blue body and could miraculously swim several feet below the lake without scuba equipment. At the time, I left my husband, came to ground zero, and started to teach meditation in London.

What I realized during my rebirthing sessions was that Babaji is Lord Shiva and that I had been connected to him for most of my life, in fact lifetimes—my mother taught me as a child to chant and repeat Babaji's "*Om Namah Shivaya*," the sacred *Maha Mantra* of India.

I found that I had all my wishes about reconnecting with Bhole Baba being fulfilled. A guy named Stephen, who I met at the *Kriya Yoga* initiation, introduced me to London *Aarti*. "*Aarti*" is the offering of the flame in praise and gratitude to the divine, and in this ceremony all the elements are also offered to the four directions and all the devotees. The five sacred elements: earth, fire, water, air, and ether are greatly revered in this ceremony. The *Vedas* teach us that the five elements are sacred force fields of archetypal energies that freely give of themselves to create our human bodies, nature, and our manifest universe. During the *Aarti* process, we use the elements, symbolically and actually, to purify their corresponding part within ourselves and outside in the entire environment.

This London group was composed of long-term devotees of Babaji. In the next ten years, unbeknownst to me at the time, I was going to become very close to all seven people who were the regulars at this sacred biweekly ceremony. This practice of chanting and celebrating the Goddess and the Divine Father became my lifeline through the many challenges, and the chaos and confusion of everyday living in our modern world. I had been on an accelerated path for years and yet my conscious reconnecting to this incredible Avataric energy moved me on my journey like nothing else.

On one occasion at tea, after our holy celebration, a lady named Rosie grabbed my attention. I announced to her (as I was being impulse by this voice within me) that I would be happy to initiate her into Karuna Mastery free of charge. She asked me to follow her into a quiet little room where she spontaneously started to channel Babaji for me. She informed me that Babaji wanted me to know that my connection to him was ancient and that we had worked together in many of my lifetimes. She also channeled that I was a powerful healer from Golden Ages in Egypt and that it would behoove me to reduce my consumption of Coca Cola!

During these years Amravati, Enoch, Stephen, Rosie, Neil, and I and a few others continued to represent in London the *Vishva Samaj Dharma* (what Babaji describes as universal spiritual practice). This sounds very dramatic, I know, and guess what—it was! We were united as a family in Babaji's love. When I first met the group, I thought I had nothing in common with this lot. Nothing could have been further from the truth. Babaji united us at our core like he does with all humanity; we just recognized it.

Amravati and I went on to work together for years, in spite of being "so-called competitors" as teachers of Reiki energy mastery and its many streams: having our advertisements appearing side by side in various new age magazines, exchanging teaching and learning, and even passing on students to each other. We achieved quite a high order of co-operation instead of competition in the crazy world of Reiki Master teachers. We did fire ceremonies galore in my little studio and amazingly managed to not set the place on fire. It was all very powerful, transforming spiritual practice and our beloved Babaji was guiding us the whole way.

At this time we were all going through intense processes (*sadana*) and our relationships were constantly adjusting as we were in Babaji's emotional-clearing cauldron, his melting pot of karmic processing and alchemical transmutation. This was obviously within our free will and it drove us from ecstasy to despair and then back up again to bliss—the roller coaster of the individual healing process and one that is being repeated now on a global level.

Rosie and I continued to channel Babaji for years together; this was in a very casual way like girlfriends meeting to gossip but instead we were bringing in Babaji's words and thoughts for ourselves, for others, and for planetary healing. She became one of my ace students and studied initiation after initiation of the wisdom teachings and continues to work even today with Hathor heart-opening attunements. At some point Babaji announced through my channeling that Rosie would soon begin to do morphogenic work for the planet and the heart opening of her peoples. It was a moment of great joy for me.

As I continued with the practices and continued to be initiated into many different streams of energy medicine, Babaji began to appear miraculously in the studio before me. It was awesome.

Nowadays I don't see him quite like that, I just feel his presence around me and I now see him as my own inner higher self. Our connection has all become a lot subtler through the years, and I miss the times when I saw him as an actual being separate from me, but the truth is that my current understanding helps me to experience Babaji in all beings everywhere.

After a few years of devoted practice, my longing to go to Mount Kailash, to Haidakhan became strong. Suddenly I was called—Babaji told me to ring Stephen, to book some dates, and come to my spiritual home in Haidakhan.

While I was in Haidakhan and we were chanting, Babaji would step out of his photograph in the temple and became a three-dimensional being, singing, dancing, and laughing in front of me. I could hardly believe it; I had to pinch myself at times. I am well traveled and yet I felt more at home in that little village in the Himalayas than anywhere else in the world. From the occasional terrifying roar of the wild cats, to the magic of fireflies flitting about in the evening, to the black deep silence of the nights in the ashram, waves of peace and remembrance of my incredible soul journey came to me.

Stephen was the perfect guide and companion for my sacred journey to Haidakhan and Chilianola (the mother ashram). He had traveled to Babaji's ashram in India year after year for spring and autumn *Navartri* (the nine-day celebration of the Goddess, the Divine Mother). This time we had arrived for *Gurupurnima*, which is a celebration and a series of ceremonies performed at the full moon once a year in praise and gratitude of the Guru and the Guru principle.

As it was the time of the monsoons, there were only twelve people in the ashram, and it was also the mango season, so we got to feast on this delicious fruit, which we received three times a day as *prasaad* (blessed food which has been offered first and foremost to God/Goddess).

Babaji shows his devotees many *leelas* (divine play/jokes). For instance I was very keen to meditate in the holy cave where he manifested in the 1970s across the river. To my great disappointment, I was told that Muniraji, our current guru and Babaji's successor, had forbidden all devotees from crossing the river as two people had died in recent attempts. The Gautama Ganga was in full swell and roaring as it flowed down from the Himalayas. The makeshift little chair-pulley system that took people across the river was unreliable.

The next day after our *Karma Yoga* practice, Babaji suddenly announced to me that I was to take an Italian girl named Vandana with me and go to the river. He said, "You will cross and go to my cave." I was confused and hesitant, but Vandana and Stephen were willing and so we went down 108 steps to the riverbank. I shouted across the din of the rushing waters to the Pujari, the keeper of the shrine, on the other side. He gave me a thumbs up. I got into the chair and was pulled across as it swayed back and forth in the high winds. I was very scared but I really wanted to meditate in that sacred space, and if I died on my journey to Babaji's cave, so be it. An overwhelming intense desire swept over me. I arrived safely on the other side, and Vandana was then pulled across after me. When I had asked the Pujari if Stephen, who is a tall man, could come next, he declined the request.

Vandana and I performed the most beautiful of ceremonies to the nine temples on the Gufa (cave) side, and we meditated together in Babaji's divine cave. Bhole Baba kindly allowed me to take a little stone from this sacred place in the heart of Mount Kailash with me to London. Coming back across the torrential river in the cable chair, I really faced my death fears. Foolishly I sat looking down at the water and I was swung furiously back and forth, and thought the pulley system was going to snap and I would fall into the river and be swept away. Stephen watched from his side of the river, praying crazily that the river would not take me, as he was petrified and didn't want to tell my mother in Delhi any bad news.

The whole journey was one miracle after another. Just to show me how dangerous it all actually was and how his grace always protects me, Babaji had me observe a dog jumping into the river. He was lashed left, right, and center by the ferocious undercurrents and barely made it back to the riverbank.

That night I received *Jharra*, powerful healing, from a wonderful swami who brushed across my body with peacock feathers while reciting the sacred mantra, "*Om Namah Shivaya*." He had lived at the ashram with Babaji and still had a little room just below Babaji's quarters.

One of the greatest gifts that Babaji gave me on that journey was to help me feel more connected to my fellow Indian brothers and sisters and to feel less like a brown English woman. The mountain people have a sweet simplicity and kindness in their souls and I truly warmed up to them. I also got to speak German to the German contingent and the Italians included me as one of them and renamed me Luciana. Babaji has a temple for the performance of *Aarti*, especially for the Italians in Haidakhan Ashram.

As one goes on to a deeper and deeper understanding and practicing of spiritual truth, love and simplicity, one is granted the *Siddhis* (celestial gifts). These are not given on demand and those that spend too much time showing off their *Siddhis*, in an imbalanced way, find that they have lost them. I have been born with special gifts as a child—the ability to talk to animals and to the elements and to have a knowingness of when it was going to rain and so on. However, years later I was granted new gifts and deeper and deeper amplification of the energy of being a psychic intuitive channel for the angelic realms, the Ascended Masters, and other beings working for the raising of consciousness on Earth. Connecting to the Divine Father, Babaji, consciously once again in this lifetime intensified these *Siddhis*, and the knowingness of things and energies become stronger and clearer and simpler with "Babaji Spiritual Practice." It is important not to be attached to these spiritual gifts or to chase after them.

My spiritual journey with Babaji continues.

He has requested in the last few years that I make a spiritual film in America on unity consciousness. And so it is currently coming to fruition. Out of the blue I was invited by my friend and publisher Robert Friedman to co-produce with Neale Donald Walsch, *iGod*, a documentary film about the unity within diversity of a multitude of spiritual paths. This film includes the voice of many of the spiritual leaders of America and the world, including religious leaders of different denominations and people of many walks of life. And this too is happening. The film should be out in 2013.

Since recovery from cancer six years ago, Babaji has also requested me to act as one of his grounding channels in the acceleration of American spiritual leaders and the peoples of America to a higher order of love and integrity, as he has of a few other of his trusted light workers. He has also impulsed me to continue to conduct Divine Mother and Heart Initiation and Healing across the globe.

And so the journey, the adventure, the joy, the ecstasy, the challenge, "the Oh-My-God" freak-outs and the constant joy of being with and serving my beloved Lord Shiva continue.

OM NAMAH SHIVAYA

Chapter Three

THE COMING AGE OF LIGHT

BABAJI TEACHES US TO love and serve all of humanity and assist everyone. He asks us to be cheerful, to be courteous, and to be a dynamo of irrepressible happiness. He teaches us to see God and the good in every face, and he reminds us of the great wisdom teaching: "There is no Saint without a past and there is no sinner without a future."

He recommends that we praise every soul that crosses our path, and if we cannot praise them, he suggests that we allow them to pass out of our lives. Babaji states: "Be original, be inventive, Dare, Dare and Dare some more."

Babaji guides us to stand our ground and not to imitate others. He asks us not to lean on the borrowed staff of others.

Babaji states the importance on the spiritual path of thinking your own thoughts and being your own self.

He proclaims that all perfection and all virtues of the Deity are inside us and that it behooves us to express them.

Babaji reminds us that our Savior is already within us and suggests we reveal Him/Her.

Finally, Babaji coaxes us into the remembrance that grace can emancipate us.

Let us all be like pristine spiritual roses, and though silent, we speak the language of fragrance.

Babaji states:

"I am Harmony, I am Harmony, I am Harmony.

"I am Peace, I am Peace, I am Peace within me now.

"From the Lord God/ Goddess of my Being I call forth all the Love, light, power that I am.

"I AM THAT I AM.

"I AM THAT

"TAT TVAM ASI

"I am not the field (the field being the mind, the body, and the intellect). I am the Knower of the Field—I am the Knower of the mind, the body and the intellect."

"I am everywhere—I am in your every breath. I come to help you realize unity beyond comparison and division. If you allow me, I will show you a freedom you cannot imagine. You must seek Unity from the awareness that we are all one. Seek harmony in all that you do, say, and think. I am harmony. If you are in peace, I am in peace. When you are troubled, I am troubled. When you are happy, I am happy. Be happy. Have faith; everything depends on faith and trust. So trust and relax.

"*Om Namah Shivaya*—I take refuge in God/Goddess within me.

"*Jai Maha Maya Ki Jai*—Glory be to the divine energy of the universe."

> "*Whatever path men and women travel is my path. No matter where they walk it leads to me.*"
> —The Bhagavad Gita

So I ask my readers: what do you feel? Do you feel we are going through a speeding-up of time, irrespective of our age? Do you observe that your personal dramas and the initiations with others are intensifying with each minute of each day? Are you witnessing that the collective consciousness of tribes and nations are in a state of flux and transformation, and some man-made systems and structures are collapsing?

This is certainly what I am observing and experiencing in my life, and as I visit many countries around the world, I witness these changes in the lives of a variety of humans I interact with, as an "ambassadress of the raising of consciousness" on the planet.

It is always incredibly amazing to me when people who have never heard of Babaji—in America and elsewhere—are suddenly exposed to his picture or hear a little bit about him, as I channel him or share a glimpse of his effulgence, and they allow him into their lives with childlike innocence. Suddenly they know that his grace and benediction can emancipate them from their suffering or feelings of victimhood and helplessness in a rapidly changing world.

Once again, I would like to remind you that Babaji, though referred to here as "he," is not limited to a particular body (official or otherwise). He is not limited to a specific time in human history or even to the male sex. In fact, many people have commented that I look just like him. This happens when I am overshadowed by Babaji's energy for the purposes of channeling or healing. He is Advaita, neither man nor woman, and paradoxically both at the same time; therefore, he is beyond such identities, beyond time and space, and certainly beyond body consciousness. However, he manifests time and again in human form, which changes from male to female and back to male as per divine wisdom.

He is pure transcendental being and becoming. It is beyond

words and linear understanding. The only way to approach the manifestation of All That Is in a human form is through the love of the heart, the devotional aspect of our being, or in a state of deep meditation. Here it is easier to access absolute reality—the unity consciousness that pervades all living and nonliving subjects and objects in the manifest universe.

In regard to the acceleration of time, Babaji has talked about Earth-Birth changes for eons, and particularly so as the Haidakhan Baba in the 1970s and early 80s. He called the great purification of Earth and humanity "Maha Kranti." (*Maha* means great and *Kranti* means a grand purging—the Armageddon or battle of the light and the shadow within all of us and in our outer realities.)

During the last 13,000 years of this Age of Darkness, we have brought about the pollution and destruction of our ecology and our physicality. All of the imbalance and disharmony created by humans on Mother Earth and amongst themselves has to be healed and purified, as the Earth moves from the 3rd dimension of time and space into the higher light frequencies of the 5th dimension, which is beyond time and space.

One of Babaji's greatest teachings about Maha Kranti is that, as we step closer toward the ending of the Mayan calendar in 2012, all of humanity will have to make many clear wholehearted choices about whether or not they will adopt impeccability of thought, word and deed. It is time now to decide and to choose to marry the divine with the mundane. It will no longer suffice that people say, I love God but my children come first, or my wealth comes first and so on. Humanity will divide into two groups: the one that will choose the divine 100 percent and the other that will continue to choose the world of duality, polarity and materialism. Babaji teaches us to become the detached witness of our relationships, our children, our dramas, our attachments, our appetites, our addictions and our material possessions.

Choosing the Divine, as our primary focus, does not imply having to give up everything immediately, because *the divine is in everything*. The important thing to practice is not to cling to one's possessions, relationships, and beliefs, and to be ready at any moment to jump for the divine and to let go of people, ideas, possessions, beliefs, attachments that no longer align with the Will of God.

How do we know what the will of the divine is, moment to moment? When you walk your talk and practice Babaji's truth of simplicity in thought, word, and deed and his ultimate teaching of love in thought, word and deed, you are a hundred percent aligned with divine will in the ongoing moments of now.

Trust your knowingness, trust your intuition. Babaji says be courageous and come from a space of heart-centeredness. You can allow your mind to ramble on—that is what the mind does: it doubts, fears, judges, and divides. The trick is to dis-identify with thoughts, just as the ocean does not identify with every wave as it ebbs and flows.

I would like to illustrate how the interplay of aligning my will with divine will, with spiritual impeccability as the goal, has played out in my life in current time and space. As I mentioned earlier, I chose to smile my way as best as I could (as opposed to choosing victimhood) through second-grade invasive cancer, chemo, and radiation therapy and two operations in less than two weeks. As a teacher of preventive medicine for fifteen years, I embraced with love this allopathic route as I simultaneously embraced the holistic path on my healing journey from this life-threatening disease.

When Babaji tells me to jump nine times out of ten, I jump. Sometimes, through my free will, I refuse. I find that, when I listen to his soft voice within me—which is synonymous with the voice of my heart and soul—I move into the realm of fun, magic, and mystery, of synergy and the *Siddhis* (special divine power gifts).

For instance Babaji impulsed me to sell my beloved studio—the temple where I initiated students from all over the world into the wisdom teachings and created a beautiful sacred space for myself and my friends—and I did. My family and friends all over the world told me not to do it. Once it sold, everyone then said, "What a genius you are, Rashmi; you sold just before the market froze." It is not I who am a genius; it is the synergy between my will and Bhole Baba's will working through me, which is incredible when it happens.

Two years ago Babaji said, "Go to New York, stay with your friend Frank Craven in Manhattan, and make TV shows about me. Visit just for one week." I was in a state of shock at this instruction, as I was just coming off a very tempestuous relationship with the fiery phenomenon known as "Frank." However, in spite of myself, I popped down to Trailfinders on High Street, Kensington and booked my flight. I was amazed to then experience the making of seven TV shows in eight days with Babaji as the main theme of three of them.

Babaji asked me to travel with Leonard Orr several years ago, and for Leonard and I to look after each other on soul level. As a result I had many adventures, faced many challenges, and connected to lots of wondrous souls across the globe. The Divine Mother energies have channeled spontaneously through me for the grace and benediction of a multitude of receptive individuals including Leonard Orr across the globe.

While I was selling my London flat, Babaji asked me to channel a book on the healing of the human heart: *The Divine Mother Speaks*. The book was published in September 2010 by Rainbow Ridge Books. You see when Babaji says that something is about to manifest, if I get my personality self out of the way and become a channel of his will, things manifest easily, organically, and synchronistically. Ultimately the results are harmonious, but while I am going through the process, it can be bumpy and full of lessons. The most important lesson in this creative process with Babaji, which I am both good and not so good at following, *is to trust and relax.*

The chanting of the mantra "*Om Namah Shivaya*" is not just repeating in a linear way some Sanskrit words inside your mind. These ancient Sanskrit sounds embody the resonance, the energy of the whole universe within them. This sacred chant means that God/Goddess dwells within us, as us, and we are seeking refuge at the feet of this divine energy which resides not only inside of us but simultaneously in all people everywhere—and in the trees, in the sky, in the rivers, in the birds, in the sun, and in the wind. Thus, we understand the universal law: as above so below, which corresponds to another universal law that ultimately the microcosm and the macrocosm reflect each other. The whole universe is the dance between *Shiva* and *Shakti*, the tango between the manifest and the unmanifest.

By repeating the "*Om Namah Shivaya*" mantra as part of divine spiritual practice in our daily lives, we begin to still the mind and purify it. Our thoughts, actions, and creations magically become more and more exalted, inspired, and unlimited. In this time of change and alchemy, in this era of the integration of the right and left hemispheres of our brain and the marrying of the right and left hemispheres of Gaia—Mother Earth—we will experience a lot of chaos and confusion as we move out of the darkness into an individual and collective awareness of the Age of Light.

As life speeds up, it is imperative that we balance this acceleration and the waking up of our DNA by *slowing down. Slowing down. Slowing down.*

When we meditate, we take our consciousness from its total fascination with the world without into the world within. Without this practice of being still, being quiet and observing one's thoughts, emotions, and desires, we cannot come out of suffering and restlessness into a state of supreme peace and experiential understanding that the God/Goddess is within us, outside of us, and everywhere.

If you are happy with your life as it is now, if you are thrilled with that which you create moment to moment, and if you have released past trauma and undesirable memory, then it could be said that you are in some state of meditative awareness. Ultimately meditation or mindfulness becomes part of one's waking, sleeping, eating, and walking state of beingness. It is there all the time and is a powerful way to stay in the now moments, which is where the power of All That Is resides.

Babaji says, "He who knows Him, knows himself and is not afraid to die." (*Atharva Veda*) Lord Shiva in his myriad forms impulsed the *Vedas*, which he gave to the many, many sages throughout time as they meditated on the nature of reality in ancient India.

It can be said that Lord Shiva is synonymous with the descent of Eternity into time. He/She is synonymous with all that is and the many names of God/Goddess that represent our manifest and unmanifest reality:

> *"He encompasses all things,*
> *Though He is the One.*
> *Who should know Him,*
> *Shiva the All-Compassionate One,*
> *Wins Peace forever."*
> —*Svetashvatara Upanishad*

Babaji, Lord Shiva, would like us to know him; for as we know him, we come to know ourselves as we are one with the Shiva Principle.

How is it possible to come out of our fascination and collective hypnosis of 3D reality to that State of Grace, where we can witness and experience a glimpse of the eternity of our Soul and of the vastness of the Oversoul energies?

Be still and know!

The mind has great difficulty in dealing with simplicity; its tendency is to analyze, judge, and to complicate the ultimate nature of reality which is intrinsically simple. Connecting one's attention and intention to Bhole Baba is a powerful and immediate path to the energy of now, the energy of simplicity, the energy of truth, and the energy of love.

The mind and ego wish to control and limit everything. The higher mind (call it Buddhi) is an integration of the right and left hemispheres of the brain—the marriage of the male and female principles within us—and is the holy union of logic and intuition.

Therefore, trying to control the inevitable evolution and transformation of ourselves and our planet, as we move more swiftly into the frequencies of *Satya Yuga*, the Age of Aquarius, is not in the realm of possibility. Yet my observation of humanity is that, as the energy of change intensifies, most individuals try frantically to stall the winds of transformation.

Unfortunately this tendency leads to a lot of suffering and frustration, and only amplifies the resonance of fear and limitation in one's life. The feeling of being in control is a cozy illusion. Mother Nature is in a state of rebalancing and purging herself. Many of our cultural systems and ways of being and relating no longer match the new frequencies of love and light that are bathing the planet.

Would a caterpillar struggle to stay in the chrysalis rather than choosing to become a pristine butterfly? Babaji says that it would behoove us to embrace the season of change and to rejoice in the detoxification of our inner and outer worlds. Each time you ask the question, "How?" Babaji answers, "Allow!"

Babaji informs us that there is no need to freak out as we let go of obsolete and dysfunctional patterns of relating, being, and doing things. Once we take out the old-fashioned floppy disc of behavior, we can become joyful conscious cocreators of our wondrous realities and replace the outmoded in our being with a preferred DVD of the divine, which is in resonance with the current frequencies of truth, love, and simplicity.

My observation of the current hysteria as banks collapse, the stock markets fall, and people lose jobs, is that surprisingly many amazing and positive innovations and changes are occurring as a result of this upheaval. For example the research shows that in many countries such as America, people are reducing the garbage output per person. This is due to humanity not just recycling paper and plastic but being more conscious of what we buy and the use of material objects in our daily life.

Many individuals are discovering the joy and fulfillment, along with the health benefits, of growing vegetables in their backyards. The obsession with buying and owning things and having to find a place for them is happily being reduced. There is now more time to slow down and to smell the flowers and to enjoy the little things of life that are very often free and truly satisfying.

Is not love more important than how many gizmos we own? Is not intimate time spent with loved ones of greater nourishment to the heart and soul than endlessly jumping into cars and airplanes and mindlessly going on excursions in the name of "busy-ness?" The paradigm of, "If I am busy, I am very important," will no longer work. It will lead to disease, accelerated aging, and early death. When we have a chance to get away from the rat race, it gives us an opportunity to come back to ourselves and to interact more deeply with significant others as well. Moving away from unbalanced materialism gives us a space to re-explore the divine mystery and to reconnect to the stars and the moon cycles, and to once again sit in a circle around Holy Fire to tell and listen to each others' stories. This is all a part of Heaven on Earth.

Om Namah Shivaya
Bhole Baba Ki Jai

OM NAMAH SHIVAYA

PART TWO

MAHA AVATAR BABJI
TEACHES US HERE NOW

INTRODUCTION

September 26, 2010

THE PHENOMENA, THE ENERGY field, the vibration, and the forceful power of Maha Avatar Babaji triggers the transformation and awakening of humanity or the individual, in the here-now, through an experiential opening and reinforcing of the heart energy.

In 1970 the mouth of the cave at Haidakhan suddenly seemed to open and become visible to the world of men and women. Within it miraculously manifested this beautiful 18-year-old yogic youth, meditating eternally on the temple of the within, as the Gautami Ganga River thundered down the hillside.

Satyam Shivam Sundaram
(Lord Shiva is Truth, Oneness, and divinely Beautiful).

Haidakhan Baba, also known as "Bhole Baba" or the "Simple Divine Father," manifested as this youth in Haidakhan but was not born of a woman. He has appeared in the vicinity of Haidakhan in different bodies through eons of time. He becomes visible to his sincere devotees or other aspirants on the path, who are ready for an encounter with a truly pure and direct emanation of Source. He has appeared to me many times in my studio in Kensington, London; to Russians in Russia; to the father of rebirthing, Leonard Orr, in America. His *leelas* abound all over the globe, oftentimes simultaneously in many places and for a variety of individuals. He is the same Babaji who is so beautifully described in the *Autobiography of a Yogi* and is the guru of gurus of the incredible lineage of *Kriya Yoga* gurus of whom Swami Yogananda was one.

Babaji is the Christ Yogi, and he is an unfathomable phenomenon that can only be glimpsed in part through infinite grace and sincere devotion.

He can and does manifest and unmanifest bodies on Earth at will. He is the descent of Infinite Spirit, Infinite Intelligence, and Infinite Consciousness into matter. He comes to us from time to time to facilitate our evolution and enlightenment.

Unlike many other gurus and avatars, Babaji uniquely shifts and processes the individual entity and soul of those who open up to his grace and benediction, specifically, and in complete keeping with the appropriateness of the lessons and blocks in the individual entity's lifetime and their free will. This makes his teachings beyond linear understanding and oftentimes illogical. Sometimes he takes you to an extreme of a polarity, which you are not embracing within your being, in order to whiplash the energies into a new pattern for a greater state of order. To take his words or even *leelas* too literally is to miss the boat to his ocean of grace.

He is the supreme teaching principle of the universe, the deepest compassion of source, and he prevails in all dimensions within manifest reality. His true home, however, is in the unmanifest supreme silence. Lord Shiva meditates eternally on Mount Kailash, on the roof of the world, the Himalayan Mountains, and everywhere.

Maha Prabhu Babaji is Lord Shiva and if you let him into your life, he will destroy ignorance and all that is false within you and so be careful if you ask for too much acceleration—you get it instantaneously.

Through multifarious lifetimes and my many years on the path in this one, I have had the grace to have darshan of various amazing gurus and avatars. I have asked to see and been shown beings that are fully enlightened and grounded in their bodies, here now, and yet once my very dearest Maha Guru Babaji re-entered my life, he became yet again my supreme teacher. One continues to work with Jesus, Kwan Yin, Mother Mary, Lord Melchizedek, Lord Buddha, the Goddess Hathor and various archangels. This is part of my initiatory work in the many streams of Reiki Energy Mastery, which is the understanding and application of the frequency of the many denominations of spirituality and their vibrations within the universal life force energies. These beings come through for various students during sessions of healing, psychic surgery, cellular memory release, and other shamanic healing journeys and ceremonies. (Ultimately all these beings, we and all are one.)

Babaji's teachings are incredible, single-pointed, and when following them, it feels like walking on the razor's edge of integrity and alertness on the path. I have not looked back! The journey has been exciting, exhilarating, and at times terrifying, and constantly challenging but never dull! What I love best about Babaji is his supreme sense of humor. He is the master entertainer and so oftentimes one gets shifted amidst great laughter. He lightens you up and enlightens you through the energy of divine play and comic cosmic mirth.

I would like herein to share this incredible force field of meditative wisdom with you, my fellow brothers and sisters, and Babaji has assured me that he has imbued the words in this book with energetic grace, courage, truth, simplicity, and love. This can bring an understanding of his amazing teachings or a reminder for those who are already familiar with this knowledge.

This work has the capacity, within your free will and the speed of your choosing, to give you an energetic, experiential understanding of Lord Shiva's world of love, healing, truth, simplicity, and bliss.

Om Namah Shivaya
Bhole Baba Ki Jai
Maha Shakti Ki Jai

OM NAMAH SHIVAYA

Chapter Four

LOVE IS

*The deeper your meditation and connection to your
inner-centered silence, the greater is the blossoming of
the flowers of love for self and others in the manifest
realm of your reality.*

September 27, 2010

LOVE IS AT THE CORE of Babaji's teachings. It is who he is and connecting with him brings one into immediate contact with the expanding infinite field of love consciousness. When one experiences this phenomenon, all boundaries begin to dissolve and a great awakening occurs spontaneously, miraculously, and oftentimes extremely intensely. This connection with Divine Avatar Babaji is very often all empowering, all encompassing, and it can quite easily turn the personality self and everything in one's life, upside down.

This connection could happen through hearing the "Om

Namah Shivaya" mantra, seeing a picture of Babaji, or just reading one of his books. It has also happened for some when the Avatar miraculously appears to a devotee in their own home. He could appear to you suddenly during meditation, chanting or healing, e.g. during a session of Rebirthing or Body Harmony.

Babaji is love.

Babaji is superconsciousness.

Babaji is All That Is.

Babaji is supreme nothingness.

This love is all-inclusive, all empowering, unconditional, non-judgmental, and it includes, yet is beyond, Karma and Dharma.

Babaji is the ascended master, the Christ Yogi, who will be with us until each and every one of us becomes enlightened through the frequencies of purity consciousness and until all of Mother Earth and the elements of this planet totally embody the 5th dimensional frequencies. These are the frequencies of being which are within yet beyond time and space.

LOVE

One is only capable of TRUE LOVE
And capable of recognizing TRUE LOVE
Only when one is touched
By the Divine Mother's Love.

The Divine Mother is
The True Manifestation
Of Unconditional Love.

If you are incapable of loving selflessly,
It is almost impossible for you
To recognize Divine Love.

> *Power without Love is very dangerous.*
> *Power combined with Love brings forth*
> *TRUE WISDOM.*
> —from *Haidakhan Babaji Speaks*

Babaji, are you with us here now?

Babaji: Now you know that is a silly question, dear Rashmiji. You as my devotee, my friend, and my channel through eons of time know perfectly well, in the very marrow of your bones, that I AM ALWAYS WITH YOU.

Let it be known, for those who have not yet reconnected with me: if they wish to do so out of their free will and heartfelt yearning for love, truth and simplicity, I can be invoked and that I will be present if you but ask it of me. But it is important for those that do not yet know me, to understand that I may or may not appear as I looked in the body that I donned as Haidakhan Baba in the 1970s and 80s.

I am "*Om Namah Shivaya,*" and as you know very well this means: "I seek the refuge of God/Goddess within me." It indicates that God/Goddess exists within each and every one of you, and that ultimately there is NO SEPARATION between You and Me. There is no separation, period (as you would say Rashmi).

This, dear children, you all forget on a constant basis:

LOVE IS ONENESS

YOU ARE ONENESS

THEREFORE YOU ARE LOVE

Ultimately there is only love:

I am love.

I am harmony.

For love is a very harmonious harmonic. The universe is love—a unity of verse.

Babaji, thank you for being here now. Thank you for myself and on behalf of all of humanity for being present for this dialogue, in this glorious present time, to guide us your children into the new frequencies with as much grace and ease as we can muster. Please would you illuminate for us how to effortlessly embody and become this frequency of all-encompassing love?

Babaji: Rashmiji, your name signifies the light: the sunlight and the moonlight. And so we shall now shed sun and moon illumination on the subject of love. I note that most of you continue to intellectualize the concepts of love, truth, and simplicity. It is important to remember that it is not enough to talk about love and to be in your mind with a basketful of love concepts. If you ask the devas, the archangels and myself, or any of the Ascended Masters, we shall fill you with our love. We shall give you a full experiential understanding of becoming one with All That Is.

Are you ready?

How much love can you take?

Are you willing to be courageous here, now and to release the so-called security of your mind and its control games?

Is it okay for you to allow a dissolving of your personality self and all false boundaries and to become an ocean of devotion, devotion to love—an ocean of love?

As you utter these amazing words, and as I allow myself to receive them, I feel an expansion of my energy fields to encompass "everything-ness" and "nothingness." It feels like I am in a very, very inky blue sky, a deep state of meditative awareness in which your words are like floating clouds or shooting stars, and I JUST AM pure beingness, deep experiential bliss. I assure you My Lord that I am not intellectualizing, here now, and actually I feel like I can watch this little "I" speaking to you from this vast, expansive, silent, peaceful state of awareness.

Babaji: Maybe we will allow you to have your inky blue-sky experience. Enjoy.

September 29, 2010

Dear Babaji, many spiritual aspirants are grappling with this question of self-love, how they can love themselves more deeply, how they can embody deeper states of loving their unique being-and-becoming—how to find their perfection within the many imperfections that seem to exist.

A lot of us so-called "healers" and "light workers," the earth mothers and fathers of this planet, have a dysfunctional tendency to put others before ourselves, even in situations where wisdom would dictate otherwise. I, for one, am much more comfortable helping others and easing their pain and suffering. When it comes to my own conundrums, I do spend a lot of time on self-healing and receiving maintenance healing from colleagues and master healers, but somehow I often make others a priority at the cost of my own inner balance.

You ask us to love and serve all of humanity. In your life, in the late 70s and 80s, you very much exemplified these principles of altruistic service and the endless processing of the karma of others. Could you shed light now, dear Babaji, on this issue of self-love and this balance of service to others and the equally important service to self?

Babaji: Dearest moonlight, unless you find time and space to be alone, to be silent, to be with nature, to play with the children, to connect to the rivers and the clouds, and to do nothing and be everything, there is no chance of self-love or love, or even service to others. Without creating space to recharge to the center of your being, which is ultimately the center of the cosmos—the manifest arising from the silent void—there is no energy for service to others; there is only depletion.

You do not like to hear this, my children, but the truth is that even if you know it you forget that need; everything has to begin from the center of your being which is within you. If you do not make time and space to connect and become at-one with this center, which again is within you, the outer reality of your life is destined to be an ongoing chaotic cacophony. Therefore, you will find that I, your dearest Lord Shiva, spend all of my time eternally meditating on the unmanifest and the manifest that springs from it on Mount Kailash above Lake Mansarovar in Northern Tibet. I am meditating everywhere and nowhere.

As I keep repeating to you dear ones, the strengthening of the anchor, at all times, to the very core of your being, is of supreme importance on this path. The deeper your meditation and connection to your inner-centered silence, the greater is the blossoming of the flowers of love for self and others in the manifest realm of your reality.

It is also of great import, as you have been taught many times, to happily and totally let go of your conditioning as it becomes relevant—to release it from your life, moment to moment. When you are in school, it is okay to listen to your teachers most of the time. However, I observe that these voices of authority from the past—be they your teachers, parents, bosses, and so on—continue to regurgitate, vibrate, and navigate the spaceship of your life, even in the here and now. This is oftentimes at the cost of your inner knowing moment to moment.

Releasing the thoughts and beliefs of people, places, and things that no longer serve you, leads to a deeper self-love and an incredible lightness of being, of a freedom that is beyond the intellectual understanding of high truth.

Lastly, on the subject of self-love, may I remind you that there is only one consciousness that has become planets, places, people, plants, passions, and all that is. Ultimately, the self does shine everywhere and nowhere as a Supreme Oneness. This is the truth of the nature of your reality beyond the veils of *Maya* and separation. In this deep state of samadhic understanding, the love of self is not separate from the love of another. All is one, all is love. Come out of the trance of being mesmerized by the dance of *Maya*.

Thank you, Babaji. When you speak, I lose the words and go deep into the energy of oneness, the dance of chiti Shakti (energetic consciousness), and the intense space of meditative bliss. Thank you for imbuing this book and the words within it with your sacred energy of alchemical transformative potency.

Dear Babaji, living and teaching in the West as I do, I find that even some of my most talented colleagues continue to hanker after a methodology in the pursuit of spiritual understanding, wisdom, and unity conscious. Generally speaking Babaji, the Western mind does not find it easy to let go of control, which involves letting go of the mind and making the heart and the wisdom energy of higher discernment in charge. In general, it is extremely challenging for the Western psyche to naturally allow deep, intuitive, inner knowingness without a need for large dollops of judgment, evaluation, analysis, and mind chatter.

Babaji: There are many paths to a deep state of love consciousness. The most powerful is the path of *Bhakti Yoga*, the yoga of devotion, where the Sadguru becomes the beloved and is honored and worshipped with wholeheartedness and deep reverence.

In *Bhakti Yoga*, as you know dear ones, the practices of chanting *Kirtan* and Aarti bring you easily, spontaneously, and oftentimes instantaneously into profound states of heart opening and oneness. The Krishna path is mostly about *Bhakti Yoga*, dancing to and with the divine within one's being and through one's body, and also bringing you into states of no-mind and deep, ecstatic, transcendental love. All forms of sacred music and high-energy sound form an instant bridge between the divine and the profane. The Sufis exemplify these states of deep referential bliss and unity heartedness.

Thank you, blessed one. I know whole books could be written about this one subject, but do you have any final words.

Babaji: Yes, dear one, I would like to remind you that love is not something to be just talked about, analyzed, evaluated, and thought about until kingdom come.

LOVE IS.

Love is not a doingness, it is a beingness.

Love is an *allowance* of the natural energy of oneness, which surrounds you and is a part of All That Is. This is an allowance at the deepest inner level, an allowance that is unconditional and involves moment-to-moment spontaneous, loving action and as Satya Sai Baba says, "The hands that work are greater than the hands that just worship." The love frequency has to be matched in thought, word, and deed, and as you know dear ones, actions speak much louder than words and sentiments. But if you fall into the trap of constantly evaluating whether something is loving or not, instead of allowing natural spontaneous, loving, right action moment to moment, you will find yourself out of love's flow and caught in the quagmire of the mind.

I AM LOVE, YOU ARE LOVE, ALL IS LOVE.

When you experience the polarity of love—be it fear, conflict, impatience, war, hatred, judgment, or prejudice—just remember that you have created a block to that which you are, which is love. This occurs through your fascination and continued engagement with your mind. It causes an immediate block to the experiential beingness of the force field of love, which is naturally in the here and now at all times.

I know for most of you, it STILL feels like separation, judgment, and negative states are the reality and that peace, love, compassion, and serenity have to be worked and fought for, and they can only be achieved through great effort and struggle. This, however, is not the case. Quite the opposite is true!

It is so simple!

Meditation is the key. You have to find time to be quiet, to be silent, and to observe your mind, your body, and your intellect. As this state of contemplation becomes an intrinsic part of your inner makeup, you will find yourself moving into deeper and deeper oceans of the energy of love.

Love is not a concept of the mind and ultimately love cannot be truly understood by the mind. The mind can act as a bridge at times to the understanding of love, but the truth is that love is experiential and ultimately beyond definition.

I would like it to be known that, if what I have just taught you here now sounds very paradoxical, it is because it is paradoxical! This is very often the nature of Universal Truth. If you choose, however, to become very clever with its definitions and if you decide to continue to stubbornly stay in the realm of your mind, as per free will, I Lord Shiva will allow you to step into the arena of cause and effect.

The greater wisdom is the feeling of my teachings and meditation on the words, their frequency and vibration. I also encourage experimenting with what is suggested: to come to your own experiential understanding of the deeper essence of your love nature.

Also dear ones, you may choose whether to love from a limited spectrum which would be, for example: I love myself, my family, my friends, and my country; or to love from a much broader perspective that encompasses the highest good of all things and everyone everywhere.

As you deepen your inner enlightenment, you will begin to encompass All That Is in your formulations, and your comings and goings, to ultimately even include the well-being of the people that oppose you, or your so-called "foes." Please don't mistake this with being a "yes" man or woman, or releasing the wisdom of inner discernment, or of the right to have boundaries and to say no.

Finally if you keep things simple, if you keep your mind simple, you simply become love, which is "all that is" in the first place!

OM NAMAH SHIVAYA

Chapter Five

COURAGE

You cannot be a true Shiva devotee if you are not prepared to walk on the razor's edge, if you are not prepared to face your fears one after the other, and thereby overcome or transcend them.

Babaji, I find the world over that even people on a spiritual path of one kind or another, still try and please others in the name of so-called unconditional love. I observe that many of your devotees and the devotees of other powerful enlightened beings chant mantras, perform yagnas, and participate in satsang, and yet continue to be afraid of offending their friends and families, even when this servility on their part leads to a total compromising of their deepest truth, love, and integrity.

Sometimes, a spiritual aspirant walks their talk in one area of their life, while they continue to sacrifice their integrity in the name of keeping the peace, which shows a total lack of courage.

I find that few people will speak their truth in a crowd, particularly if their expression of integrity is in conflict with the views of the mob. We are past December of 2012, and yes people are waking up and great miracles of conscious connection are occurring, but this lack of courage that I am pointing out, here now, continues to be chronic and widespread. How can we shift out of this fear of being and embracing who we are, or of loving others through having to say no to them, or even at times oppose the views or behavior of the people we love?

Babaji: Dear humanity, I have come to you through the ages, and each time I have taught you about the tremendous power of the energy of courage. You cannot be a true Shiva devotee if you are not prepared to walk on the razor's edge, if you are not prepared to face your fears one after the other, and thereby overcome or transcend them. In esoteric wisdom you are often taught about the path of the peaceful warrior, the spiritual warrior. This voyage through darkness to light is where the sadguru can help greatly. The word guru means from darkness to light. The outer guru takes one to the inner temple, in which resides the inner guru principle—the "I AM" Presence, the "I am Shiva" presence, the "I am All That Is" energy, and the void of a deep state of meditative consciousness.

I AM THE GURU OF GURUS.

It is imperative for human beings now to take responsibility for their lives, their words, their deeds, and their co-creations. The ability to respond from conscious-centered awareness comes from keeping a part of your attentive consciousness in the center of your being which is empty, silent, and in the unmanifest realm.

The energy and the invocation of Durga Mata, of Lord Shiva, of Lord Hanumanji, or of Archangel Michael instantly bring you into a state of courageous moment-to-moment awareness and intuitive, centered knowingness.

Once you have accessed this state and become firmly anchored in it, you no longer have to worry about when to speak and when to be quiet, when to fight the good fight and when to harmonize with others through gentle silence or peaceful discussion. In each moment of now, you just calmly or forcefully, as the case may be, follow your inner guidance and wisdom, and you will not be afraid of the opinion of others or offending others, or trying to please or manipulate them into your way of being or thinking.

THE TRISHUL SYMBOL

Meditating on the trishul will take you to a deep place of courageous right thought, word, and deed.

When looked upon as Lord Shiva's weapon of awareness, the trishul destroys the *illusion* of the three worlds: the physical world, the world of our ancestors, and the world of the mind. All three are transformed by me through the so-called "destruction" into a single non-dual plane of existence, which is bliss alone.

Now you see dear ones, that there is no true love from a profound spiritual point of view without embracing the energy and practice of deep courage. Love is not for the weak-hearted. The *Shiva* path is not for the weak-hearted. *Samadhi* is not for the weak-hearted.

Especially now, as we move beyond 2012 and the great changes that we all face. At the same time, I feel that so many of us, even the so-called spiritually enlightened, are clinging to the past, to the sorrow and sadness of the past.

Babaji: I observe that most of humanity is feeling a vast amount of fear, stress, and worry in this ending of the *Kali Yuga*, which involves tremendous change. I encapsulate the energy that triggers deep courage in your hearts and minds, here now, in these words as I speak them to you. You cannot cross the bridge of fire and water and endure the storms of accelerated transformation without inculcating deep fearlessness in your mind, body, and soul.

Your *Atma* (soul) is essentially fearless.

Move forward as a spiritual warrior with peace and love and find the energy to speak your truth with courage and to be silent when necessary, with an equal amount of bravery and single-pointedness.

There will be no self-realization and moving into *Satya Yuga* without a total and absolute level of integrity, where your thoughts match your words, which then match your deeds.

Babaji, I always love your energy of intense razor-like truth that cuts through conditioning, secrets and misinformation on the spiritual path. Thank you for amplifying the energy of bravery and love in our hearts through this dialogue, in this now time, when we are all being intensely challenged to let go of lifetimes of samskaras, memories, attachments, desires, people, and places that cannot come with us, as the light we be and are becoming undergo accelerated transformation into higher unified consciousness.

It is exciting that apparently Muniraji has said that you have once again manifested in a physical body on earth, here now, to guide and lead us, your sincere devotees, to a higher octave of our oneness with all that is.

I know that, ultimately, you are not a body even though you materialize and dematerialize in one or several physical forms on earth, from time to time.

Could you share with us any information about how to access your energy more powerfully here now, whether it be a bodily form of the oneness that you represent and are, or your energy in its transcendental state, so that we can reduce our fear and come into our knowingness, with the serenity of moving forward in trust and moment-to-moment awareness.

Babaji: My children of the light, you know very well that the darkness, the fear, and the ignorance are illusionary. However, you continue to be completely mesmerized and caught up in the drama of *Maya*: of polarity and the demons of fear-based living and being. I have taught you to repeat the *Maha Mantra*, "*Om Namah Shivaya*." It is there to purify your mind and bring it to stillness—a centeredness that exists at all times, even as you interact with the world.

You know also dear ones, if you allow yourself to connect to an image of me that makes your heart sing, or even in some cases one that may be frightening, you will be able to access my energy with the purity of your heart's intention with ease and grace.

Just chasing after my body form as the ultimate truth is missing the point of that which I am. As you know dear ones, I am not the body; I am Supreme Being containing the energy of the manifest and the unmanifest at the same time. Ultimately, I am beyond time and space and the truth is that "you and I are one." I have full consciousness of unity, of my I AMness, which you have forgotten. You now are beginning to remember, once again, as you wake up to who you are.

I am the mirror of who you be.

There is no point in saying that you are a devotee of Babaji, of Lord Shiva, while being out of integrity in thought, word, and deed.

It is useless to talk about practicing universal dharma while not having the courage to stop clinging to those things, ideas, and people that your inner knowingness, through me or from within yourself, is asking you to release from your reality.

Whether I appear to you in bodily form or transcendentally or symbolically, it is all the same. It is ultimately you connecting to the deepest part of your "I AM" presence which, as you know, is within you.

The cave in which I manifested miraculously as an 18-year-old youth (not born of a woman), on the *gufa* (cave) side of the Guatami Ganga in Haidakhan, is symbolic of the deepest part of your inner space. This is your "temple of the within," which is at one with all that is manifest and which is ultimately supreme, unmanifest, "isness," and silence.

Ask me and I will answer.

Call me and I will appear.

Be sincere and my many gifts shall unfold in your life.

Heartfelt sincerity is a key to accessing me.

Your purity of heart will determine how much of my presence you will be able to bear without going into total terror.

The terror only arises from a heart and a mind that are moving in different directions to truth, love and simplicity.

If you only pray and do not work for the service of mankind, you are not a true devotee of mine.

If you only work and do not bring in the reverence of the divine (which is All That Is) through sacred conversation with the divine (which is prayer), celestial singing to the divine (which is *Kirtan*), ecstatic dancing in gratitude and praise to the divine (which is celebration), then you are not really following that which I have come to teach you.

Thank you, Babaji. It is so easy for us to forget the simplicity of your wondrous teachings. I suppose what we have to remember, Maha prabuji, is that we eat every day for the whole of our lives and so why should we forget to chant every day, to show praise and gratitude every day to the sacred elements: earth, water, fire, air, and ether, and to achieve unity consciousness from an ocean of devotion through repeating the Maha Mantra, "Om Namah Shivaya," or for that matter any mantra that resonates with our hearts.

Babaji: My little *chelas*, devotees (a little joke since there is no one leading and no one following at the highest level of truth), the biggest fear, in third-dimensional reality on earth, is the demise of the body, the physical form. This is also caused by a deep fear of change.

For some of you, through the ages, I have recommended actually meditating at the cremation ground until you begin to have the realization that ultimately you are not the body. You are a transcendental being and becoming, and your soul energy continues its journey in another form and then another and another.

If you want to transcend deep fear, then be with the fear, accept it, release denial, and look at it in the face.

Keep meditating on the cause of the terror or anxiety, or keep looking at it and you will find that, if you breathe into the experience and allow it, you will transcend this angst and come to a place, on the other side of the fear tunnel, of great peace and in some cases, bliss.

The only way to overcome the fear of the unknown is to face the unknown, step into it and have a thorough experience of it. It is rather amusing for me to observe this phenomenon amongst my human children.

For of course when one experiences the unknown, it transforms and becomes the known. I, Babaji, find this extremely funny, don't you?

One observes that many of you, like my dear Rashmi, are at times captivated with making themselves totally frightened through their supremely vivid imagination as a form of excitement and entertainment.

Rashmiji, you and your fellow brothers and sisters may continue this egocentric form of behavior as the divine grants you full free will.

Yes, yes, "the Rash one," I can hear your mind asking me how to break this so-called bad habit; for as you have seen for yourself, my channeling angel, once you co-create creative excitement in your life, your need to manifest chaos as nightmares, in your case, is automatically released.

Ultimately the supreme silence that you be is neither excitement nor a lack of it. It just is.

P.S. So with fear, remember to accept it, embrace it and let it become one with the light which you are within, and thereby transmute it. A great example of the fear becoming bliss is my beloved *chela*, Leonard Orr's cold water rebirthing. Rashmi, Amravati, and many others have experienced immersing themselves bit by bit into freezing cold water, and going through pain and terror and then coming into states of bliss and ecstasy—the polarity. Powerful practice!

OM NAMAH SHIVAYA

Chapter Six

I AM HARMONY

Without meditation there is no harmony. With ecstatic heartfelt song, dance, and praise to the divine within and without, harmonic states are accessed and anchored with ease and grace. Why not join Shiva's dance of ecstasy and vital beingness?

Babaji: I am harmony, I am harmony, I am harmony!

My darling Rashmi and my dearest Amravati have just meditated and have allowed themselves to swim in the energy of the *Maha Rhudram*. I will let them continue and answer the questions in their hearts if not on their lips.

This *Maha* chant is in praise of the many aspects and energies with which I, Lord Shiva, embody and dance as I unfurl manifest reality through my eternal meditation on Mount Kailash in Northern Tibet, in the Himalayan Mountains—the roof of the world. This chant takes you into a state beyond the mind, to the depth of the inner core of your awareness, which is essentially empty, silent, and harmonious. In this inner temple of harmony and nothingness, you are able to access your immortal being and becoming with tremendous ease and grace, if you but allow it.

You are harmony. As I have said before, you and I are one.

I am in your every breath.

I am in earth, water, fire, air, and ether.

I am the primordial sound AUM.

Sacred sound, such as the chanting of the Vedic texts like the *Rhudram*, take you immediately to your transcendental self, to your *Shiva* self which is within you, if you but allow it.

Are you ready?

How much of my presence can you take in your life?

The divine is beckoning. Can you bring yourself to enough peace and quiet to hear the celestial call of the divine within you?

I am the Universe. I am therefore the Unity of Verse. Lord Shiva is a synchronicity and a synergy of a myriad of energies all coming together as the pure, harmonious song and dance of oneness and love.

I am the energy of courage and fearlessness, of truth, simplicity, and love, and ecstatic song drumming, and the dance of *Nataraja*.

As you become one with the *Maha Mantra*, "*Om Namah Shivaya*," you align yourself with the energies of *Shiva*, and these vibrations emanate from the "Temple of Silence," which is within and spread into the body, mind, intellect, and aura. As this happens, you become eternal being and becoming—beyond time and space, yet happy to dance within the illusion of time and space.

YOU BECOME IMMORTAL.

On the subject of immortality, I, Avatar Babaji, would like to state that physical immortality is just one part of the deeper understanding of being eternal. Ultimately, as I keep reiterating, you are not the body. Your energy continues beyond the endless cycles of life and death.

Intrinsically, you are anchored in the supreme reality of the unmanifest from which springs forth manifested worlds, bodies, life-times, karmas, and *gunas* (qualities of the soul).

It is okay and totally possible to live in the same physical body for thousands of years, which is well illustrated by me and my beloved entity Bhartriji, immortal yogi and king of 2000 years.

However, to become too attached to any physical form is not the highest esoteric truth within the school of Lord Shiva. Supreme reality is beyond worlds and bodies. It exits in intrinsic silence, the unmani-fest, nothingness.

For you to merely understand this truth intellectually is missing the point. You need to understand these words in an experiential way, in a way that allows the mind to become totally quiet so that the energy behind the words can be experienced.

It is interesting to note that since my appearance as Bhole Baba in Haidakhan in the late 1970s and early 80s that you have forgotten what Lord Shiva represents more than anything else. Can you guess what that is? MEDITATION! If you meditate and make this a regular part of your spiritual practice, then I will facilitate the merging of your third eye with the third eye of Lord Shiva. This is the energy vortex between your eyebrows that connects you to the all-seeing, all-know-ing, and all-pervasive vision of supreme beingness.

Let it be known that you can reach this deep space of inner medi-tative bliss and emptiness through ecstatic chanting: a total absorp-tion of oneself, be it into the yoga of work (*Karma Yoga*), while reciting the name of the Lord, or other practices.

Without meditation there is no harmony. With ecstatic heartfelt song, dance, and praise to the divine within and without, harmonic states are accessed and anchored with ease and grace. Why not experiment? Why not join Shiva's dance of ecstasy and vital being-ness? Why not allow the melting away of conditioning and reactive, robotic states of being through offering all your thoughts, words, and deeds to the divine? This divinity is, as I keep saying, everything and nothing, or ALL THAT IS and the unmanifest.

It is time now to come out of the cacophony of *Kali Yuga*, the age of ignorance and darkness, the age of extreme materialism and separation. It is time to embrace the holy harmonics of being a whole and complete integrated energy field of beingness, which creates an incredible melody through the spheres within manifest reality. If you see yourself as part of the organic wholeness of a unified field of consciousness, you can create harmonic realities.

When you choose to be separate and for or against things, as opposed to seeing the all-inclusiveness of love, you cause your own pain, your own suffering, and your own isolation. In this disharmonious state, you are going against, rather than with, the flow of the river of life. It is time to wake up. It is time to be brave and change bad habits. It is time to become that which you already are in every area of your beingness: pure experiential harmony.

When the deepest inner core is centered in silence and the unmanifest, your personality self, your body, your thoughts, your words, and your actions become synchronistic, synergistic, and harmonious. Then you are one with the abundant flow of time, energy, money and love in your life—within and without.

I AM HARMONY, I AM HARMONY, I AM HARMONY.

OM NAMAH SHIVAYA

Chapter Seven

OM NAMAH SHIVAYA

Chanting the "Om Namah Shivaya" within, or singing it aloud, helps you to bring the mind to a place of crystal clarity, where the mind becomes like a still pool and all unconscious predispositions begin to reveal themselves in this serene still water.

I know how sacred sound calls us to the divine within us, but for those particularly in the West who often come from a mental understanding, can you explain the significance of this Shiva mantra?

Babaji: The meaning of the *Maha Mantra*, "*Om Namah Shivaya*" is extremely deep and is understood, as usual, from a feeling point of view rather than just a mind understanding.

"*Om Namah Shivaya*" means:

I love myself.

I honor myself.

God/goddess dwells within me, as me.

Another meaning is: "I seek refuge at the feet of the god/goddess within me."

Om is the primordial sound of the universe. It is the energy of the unity and oneness of the universe beyond separation.

Namah is the invocation of the *Shiva* principle in this case.

Shivaya is the female aspect of the *Shiva* energy, and *Shiva* is the male aspect of the *Shiva* principle. *Shiva* means the same shining pristine all-pervasive all-knowing self that resides at the core of all beings and within the entirety of creation everywhere. I would like to clarify for you that this *Shiva* principle exists within each and every one of you, but it is not a separate energy in each individual or a different flavor in me and another flavor in you. At the deepest core, when I say that you and I are one, the *Shiva* in you and I are one. The difference is: I am in full conscious awareness of my I AM presence, within time and space, and beyond time and space, and YOU HAVE FORGOTTEN.

As you re-remember your *Shiva* self, as you re-remember the unity of all that is, as you make this unity an experiential moment-to-moment awareness, you become *Shiva* fully realized. The whole universe opens itself up to you in joy, co-creation, and a letting go or destruction of that which no longer serves your higher good, moment to moment.

It is important to keep one's attention and one's heart centeredness during the repetition of this mantra. With practice a true aspirant becomes more and more single-pointed in the energy of the sacred sounds within and without. To just repeat *"Om Namah Shivaya"* like a mental robot will lead to a limited reaping of the fruits and gifts of this discipline. A time will come when the mantra becomes an intrinsic part of your inner makeup and is always present and affecting your mind, your body, and your intellect. When the mind becomes purified and simple and quiet through this powerful practice, it naturally marries itself to the energies of the heart, and the rose fragrance of your heart-centeredness will infuse all your energy bodies, your aura, and the universe. Patience and practice and determined *sankalpa* (intention) are of utmost importance, dear ones.

When you combine the practice of chanting the mantra silently within, while performing any so-called mundane work: for example, washing the dishes or doing the laundry, you exalt the entire process to a high vibrational frequency. Even the simplest tasks now become joyful prayerful sacred activities, in which the fruits, the bliss and the work are naturally and effortlessly offered up as service and praise and gratitude to the divine. To re-remind you: this divine principle is within you, not just in a picture of me or a *murti* (statue) of me or a transcendental experience of me or any other aspect of my celestial energy.

I observe that many of you have the faulty understanding that you are superior to the rest of the human race because you are practicing my Way. To strut around like a spiritual peacock with great disdain for lesser so-called "ignorant" mortals IS NOT APPROPRIATE. To think that you are purer than those not practicing a conscious spiritual path is also a form of ego-based, spiritual prejudice.

Having said this, it is obviously all right for you to follow the quiet voice within you for when to move with the crowd and when to be alone and be quiet. Spiritual balance and being grounded are the keys.

It is better for you to repeat the mantra with heartfelt feeling and devotion than to allow the mind to think, worry, doubt, and indulge in deep analysis and in general chronic stress.

If you say to me that you want to cling to the habits of the mind and you are not willing to embark on a conscious, spiritual journey into the temple within, I say to you, "As you sow, so shall you reap." It is your choice. It is time to wake up, as I keep telling you, and you have to take responsibility for the cause-and-effect triggers that occur from your choices moment to moment. This includes your unconscious choices. Chanting the *"Om Namah Shivaya"* within, or singing it aloud, helps you to bring the mind to a place of crystal clarity, where the mind becomes like a still pool and all unconscious predispositions begin to reveal themselves in this serene still water.

Keeping awake all night long on full-moon nights, as a form of sleep fasting, is potent Shiva practice especially when combined with my *Maha Mantra*.

Thank you, Babaji, for all this wondrous energy behind all your celestial soul-empowering words. When we performed the fasting from sleep practice, it changes our habitual patterns completely and helps to align the energies of one's beingness into a new and potentially more vital and creative pattern.

I find that when I am in Haidakhan during Kirtan/Bhajan time (chanting), and during Aarti, in your temple of accelerated intense spiritual energy, that I go into instantaneous states of ecstatic bliss and divine mirth.

OM NAMAH SHIVAYA

Chapter Eight

HUMOR

*For those of you that feel spirituality and the path to
self-realization have to be a serious business, let me tell
you that I, Bhole Baba, prefer to teach you as often as I
can with the frequency, the energy of laughter.*

Babaji: Looking at the lot of you, from our vantage point as Ascended
Masters, we are rather amused when you take the dramas of your life
so seriously. Seeing the divine *leela*, or divine play, in everything is
powerful esoteric wisdom. I love to teach you through the energy of
humor, not just because it is so funny but also because it is in keeping
with the essential nature of your so-called "reality."

*This is what I love most about my interaction with you, Babaji, or
shall I say what is left of it, as you and I become more and more part
of the same beingness. In this lifetime when I reconnected with you so
powerfully fifteen years ago, you would appear at the top of my stairs in
the studio as a vast figure of white light and love and, as time went on,*

you would appear to me on airplanes and street corners, or in the park, and all in different human forms. In this current time, our connection has become more subtle as the "you and I" of things has begun to disappear and, in the place of this "I-separate-from-you consciousness," you have become my own inner higher self, my all-knowing self, the voice of divinity within me.

You have taken me on this wondrous journey from the without to the within with great grace, amazing ease and most importantly, large dollops of incredible humor. And this has made even the scariest and most challenging moments on the unique Shiva voyage light and bearable, and oftentimes I see the whole drama as major comedy!

Babaji: Glad to be your court jester, Madam! As Haidakhan Baba, I loved spending time with the children because they epitomize the energies of play, fun, humor, and lightness. To me you are all like little children, except sometimes, when you become too serious and you become overly identified with so-called "pain and suffering."

This is when I have to come in and tickle you with the feathers of the divine dusting brush. For example, as Rashmi was walking here, in a state of total huff and puff about channeling my book, she was feeling that I have asked her to be homeless, jobless, and without a romantic partner. I decided to tickle her.

That's right! Thank you for reminding me, Babaji. As I was listening to my iPod, moments before entering the great channeling chamber of Amravati's flat, you started dancing this wild, crazy Latin American jive, and it was really funny seeing you wearing a dhoti in the middle of a street in cold autumnal London. I know it was silly, but it did the trick, pulling me out of my self-pity. I saw how ridiculous I was being, when I had chosen every step of this incredible journey I am on with you, Babaji, my best friend, and was ready once again to take responsibility for it.

Babaji:
My dear children keep things light,
keep them bright,
and that way you won't get into a fight,
and just remember you don't always have to be constantly right.

For those of you that feel spirituality and the path to self-realization have to be a serious business, let me tell you that I, Bhole Baba, prefer to teach you as often as I can with the frequency, the energy of laughter.

OM NAMAH SHIVAYA

Chapter Nine

INTUITION AND DOUBT

Following your intuition and the voice of your soul, you know
very well requires: being silent, being alone, being with nature,
and being still from time to time . . . Unless you make time
and space away from mind chatter, you will miss the subtle
whispering of your "all knowing" self from within you.

Babaji, as a teacher of the spiritual way and metaphysical wisdom of
many different streams of esoteric understanding, I find that many of my
students—and human beings in general—have great difficulty in discern-
ing between the voice of their mind and the subtle whisperings of their
higher self or heart energy. Also, they struggle with their intuition and
then have an even greater challenge trusting where the voice of inner
knowingness is guiding them. Could you shed your brilliance on these
issues of mind, heart- knowing and doubt?

Babaji: As you know my little ones, you are becoming more and
more intuitive in these end days. Following your intuition and the
voice of your soul, you know very well requires: being silent, being

alone, being with nature, and being still from time to time. If you ask, you shall receive, as the Bible tells you. Your mind, however, likes to fool you into expecting answers to come in a particular way, from a particular person, and so on. Once you have asked, you have to create a quiet space and give it time to allow the answer to come forth. Unless you make time and space away from mind chatter, you will miss the subtle whispering of your "all-knowing" self from within you.

Sometimes the answer could come as a picture, a symbol, or an idle remark from a close friend. As long as you have made an intentional effort to become acquainted with the energy of your mind and its favorite dialogues, and the energy of your soul wisdom in its stillness and subtlety, you will be able to decipher which voice belongs to which part of you. If there is doubt, this is the mind. Your intuition is a knowingness beyond doubt. As you know, Rashmiji, a little bit of intelligent doubting is always good on the spiritual path. This doubting can actually be discernment about being too naive and overly gullible in accepting the possible misinformation from false teachers (although even a false teacher will ultimately teach you something, even if it is not to make the same mistake again).

Are you willing to learn?

The doubting of your intuition and your knowing self, which is ultimately beyond conditioning, authority, and logic—although it may contain elements of the above—is one of the many mind tricks used to trip you up on your journey back from Soul to Oversoul, as I would say: *Atma* to *Paramatma*. The answer that your knowing self gives you is oftentimes in conflict with the agenda of your mind. Your mind wishes to cling to the known, to control, to limitation, and to doubt and fear, in order to make you separate, isolated, and disconnected. The goal of your knowing self, your higher self, is to see a much larger picture that possibly takes into consideration qualities inherited from past lives, the goals of your soul, and universal law.

Once you become conscious of the nature of your mind and its thinking process, and you connect to the goals of your soul through meditation, prayer, silence, *Jappa*, and *Kirtan*, you will be well acquainted with the different colors, qualities and flavors of these two distinctly different energies operating within you. Some choices can then be very safely and automatically made within the realm of the mind. Other choices may require you to go deeper within and see the larger picture of where your soul's journey is wanting to take you and how that fits in, or is in complete opposition with, the agenda of your personality self.

This is wisdom: becoming acquainted with the many colors and flavors operating within you. Be the *Sakshi* (the witness) when observing your inner atmosphere. Let go of any judgments or resistance to acceptance of that which is operating within you. Watch it, accept it and, once you do this, you can come to a new level of choice based on a higher paradigm.

IF YOU CHOOSE TO, OF COURSE!

If you continue what psychologists would call a form of schizoid behavior, where you are pretending to come from soul-motivation while actually the ego-self is ruling the roost, you will trigger karma, suffering, pain, disease, and early death. So if you really wish to experience an aspect of your personality-self that your soul-self knows is harmful, then it is better to have a full experience of whatever it is your mind hankers after, than to do a little of this and a little of that and create a total confusion of your inner energetic self, within and therefore without.

I note that you continue to feel that things happen to you from the outside, whereas your reality occurs from the within to the without, not from the without to the within. Let it be noted that if you do decide to indulge in the addictions and predispositions of the personality-self, which are in direct opposition with your soul goals, then you must take full responsibility for the law of cause and effect as it triggers in your life.

So often, I watch you indulging in what your soul knowingness knows to be illusionary and delusionary, feeling that somehow the divine is not watching; that somehow, you have managed to sneak around the law of action-reaction. Come out of this delusion, dear ones!

Remember if your goal is kindness, and if your thought, word, and deed have an ultimate resonance of compassion, then your harvest is one of kindness and compassion. If your goal is within the narrow spectrum of me, mine, I, my family—to the exclusion of the broader perspective and oneness of all things—then you are choosing from a frequency of win/lose as opposed to win/win, or the higher good of all everywhere. Choosing from a narrow perspective gives you a limited harvest. Choosing from the perspective of the highest good of all concerned at all times, will give you the harvest of synergy, synchronicity, ecstasy, moment-to-moment celebration, and peace within, no matter what is happening on the outside.

Here is an affirmation for you, my dear ones:

KNOW THAT YOU KNOW.

I KNOW THAT I KNOW (this is not the knowing of the ego-self).

The knowing of the ego-self normally comes from the language and the energy of the mind. The knowing of the higher self, the I AM presence, usually comes through the feeling body, and in some cases through what humans call the gut instinct. Following this knowing body leads to spontaneous right action, effortless being, and integrity of thought, word, and deed, moment to moment.

OM NAMAH SHIVAYA

Chapter Ten

ACCELERATED TRANSFORMATION

The more you cling to the materialistic or linear under-standing of your reality, the more you remain stuck in the energy of the previous age, which is now beginning to recede and make way for the Age of Light.

Babaji, my most beautiful being of love and compassion, can you shed some light and wisdom on one of the most critical issues facing humanity here now, both individually and collectively—the accelerated transformation occurring on earth in this now moment. I find that though I am very good at jumping off cliffs (metaphysically speaking), that even I manage, from time to time, to go into a tailspin when having to let go of the familiar situations that were known and therefore comfortable. In general most of my fellow brothers and sisters, I find, are in deep terror of change and uncertainty.

As we know, that in order to cope with this fear, most human beings tend to control their mind and body and their environment in a desperate effort to create the cozy illusion of certainty and control. In this now moment, as we experience the speeding-up of the changeover to the higher harmonics, how can you help us cope and bring ease and grace into moving forward to deeper trust and serenity?

Babaji: Rashmiji, you have a wonderful knack of seeing where energy gets stuck, and the collective energy of humanity, here now, is simultaneously stuck yet moving rapidly forward, on this issue of acceptance, allowance, and trusting change.

One of the biggest problems, we the Ascended Masters observe amongst humanity, here now, is that oftentimes you are individually and collectively coping with the accelerated transformation rollercoaster using old tools and paradigms from the Age of Pisces, the Age of Darkness.

The trick is to be aware of this tendency and chose the new tools on the block—the keys of the Age of *Satya Yuga*. What does all this mean? I can hear your minds asking this question. The more you cling to the materialistic or linear understanding of your reality, the more you remain stuck in the energy of the previous age, which is now beginning to recede and make way for the Age of Light.

This literally means, dear ones, you are becoming lighter and you know this, but you forget to re-remember this crucial fact of your rapidly changing reality, in the here and now.

Rashmiji, you for example, are currently feeling a little depleted by the constantly changing state of your relationship with a significant other, and a part of your mind would be quite happy to use this as an excuse to not show up over the next six days for the purposes of completing the channeling this book. Currently, you are bravely choosing to continue to do my work, in spite of your mind chatter, which is trying to pull you back into the frequency of separation and heaviness—the energies of clinging and lethargy.

So well done, dear one!

Amravati is also showing up bravely in spite of the recent loss of her dear cat and other intense challenges to transcribe as Rashmi channels.

Let it be known that the two of you have been asked to participate in this sacred work as you have both spent lifetimes on the *Shiva* path, performing *yagnas*, *aarti*, meditating and listening to my will within you. Also, as teachers of Reiki masters and practitioners, it is appropriate that I wish for Rashmi to channel and Amravati to transcribe this sacred work.

In this glorious now time, all humans are becoming channels of their multidimensional being—some more quickly and clearly than others.

Thank you for your encouragement, Babaji. I have to say that it is not always easy and yet when the two of us show up, I find that the actual process of channeling your energy comes as second nature to me.

Both Amravati and I find that the energies in this space become heightened and palpable on many different levels. In fact, the energy is as powerful in the English channeling, as when we are listening at the beginning of each session to the powerful Vedantic chant of your very famous Rhudram. It is all quite incredible.

Babaji: Dear One, coming back to how to cope with accelerated change, it is important to remember that at the center nothing is happening; nothing is changing, and that the whole of this holographic reality is an illusion. Without moving into a higher, inner, deeper perspective, coping with the speeding train of change will lead to chaos, confusion, panic, and unnecessary fear and derailment.

When you see a scary film, you can enjoy getting frightened and yet in your heart you know that you are just watching a drama on the silver screen. In the same way, it behooves all of you now to remember that you are the immortal, eternal screen of unmanifest potential on which you may create what you desire, for the purposes of entertainment, learning or co-creation, or the sheer joy of creating for creation's sake.

Also, it amuses me to no end, dear ones, to observe that very often you are clinging to an old choo-choo train, like a little five year old child deprived of its favorite toy, while we, the Ascended Ones, have celestial gifts to give you that are far more expansive: such as you being able to sit on your own etheric express train and possibly zipping through the cosmos. Do you get the drift, dear ones? Why are you clinging to a limited version of yourself, no matter how comforting that might be to you, and to the perspective of your ego, when worlds upon worlds are beckoning to be discovered and experienced?

New colors of celestial crayons are being given unto you to draw a more expanded and vividly lighter picture of whom you wish to co-create yourself into being. I AM LORD SHIVA and as you know very well, I destroy the obsolete on the spiritual path in order to recreate/ co-create a new pattern of a higher paradigm for all. You must learn to be empty to receive. Feel this pulsation of the universe, its ebb and the flow. Make "being empty" okay. Then perhaps practice making "being empty" or alone as "being peaceful" or "being blissful."

To crave excitement all of the time is to burn out quickly and easily. To hanker after serenity and peace, at all times, is to miss out on the passion and dynamic pulsation of the creation of new ideas and worlds. My channel Rashmi has currently slipped into an inter-dimensional portal of energy frequency that allows for the creation of worlds. She is experiencing this currently as a vast expansive feeling like floating in a sea of clouds, which is an ocean of potential co-creative possibilities of sound, light and color.

As you said that Babaji, I zapped out of it! I would like to share here that the only way I am able to keep sane, as I keep letting go and embracing nothingness, is by balancing this intense spiritual phenomena in my life with a continued, intuitive, moment-to-moment creativity. This happens when I follow the voice of my soul and the voice of my beloved guru Maha Avatar Babaji as my own inner higher self.

Two years ago, if I had not voluntarily let go of my beloved temple, the studio in Kensington, I would not have been able to spontaneously channel at the same time the powerful book called The Divine Mother Speaks: the Healing of the Human Heart. Now, I am able to channel this book on Lord Shiva, as I consciously allow myself to watch a deep personal relationship transform rapidly, as I simultaneously make time and space for this work here now.

Babaji: It is important to repeat this knowingness: that ultimately the still place of nothingness, where nothing is changing, is the anchoring reality of the simultaneously occurring ever-changing landscapes of your inner and outer awareness.

Every time you experience deep emptiness or aloneness, and feel panicky and bereft, know that you are advancing spiritually and that you must persevere in making these states okay. Chanting the mantra, "*Om Namah Shivaya*" facilitates an easing of these symptoms of spiritual emptiness and aloneness, and as you know dear ones, so does sitting with fire, performing *Yagna*, *Kirtan*, *Aarti*, prayer, meditation, and being with nature.

Satsang and the help of a true guru, who connects you to your heart and teaches independence of choice at the same time, or the invocation of any other Being of light or love such as Jesus, Moses, or Archangel Raphael, will lift you on the wings of an eagle to a new understanding.

You may ask how to distinguish between aloneness and loneliness.

Aloneness is an expression of the spiritual nothingness that you are. By this I mean the silence, the unmanifest within you. On the other hand, loneliness is an energy of the ego that feels separate from the organic wholeness of all things. Loneliness is one of the diseases of the mind, and unfortunately the heart can also catch this virus in those that are not pursuing sincere self-realization.

Anyone who has not attained inner equilibrium, to anchor themselves in inner silence and to realize that ultimately they are nothing and nothing is actually happening, cannot pretend in any convincing way to be a great teacher or facilitator of healing and evolution. In other words, dear ones, giving up the predominant obsession with outer impression and image and connecting strongly to the inner climate, and weeding on a regular basis the garden of the within, are of prime importance on the path.

As we have said before, unless you are willing to be courageous there is no point in moving forward on the *Shiva* path. Trust and faith are of all importance.

Om Namah Shivaya
Jai Maha Maya Ki Jai

OM NAMAH SHIVAYA

Chapter Eleven

FAITH AND TRUST

*Every time distrust or lack of trust comes up, watch it,
allow it and find a way to disidentify from this energy
... The very process of watching and allowing, without
judgment, creates a space in your being.*

*Babaji, it is really ironic that I have this wonderful trust that the universe
will continue to support my spiritual princess-hood and the creative channeling of "wisdom teaching" books, making spiritual films, teaching, and
my sadhana; yet there is a dichotomy in that I have subtler and subtler
trust issues tripping me up on a pretty frequent basis. I find that humanity
continues (myself included) to have a chronic problem vis-a-vis trust and
faith, on a moment-to-moment basis. Can you help us with this issue,
here now?*

Babaji: The only way my child, as you know well, to heal this issue
of distrust is to reorient yourself, out of the realm of your Doubting
Thomas mind, into the supreme peace and quiet of your all-knowing,

all-pervasive silent Self, which is deep within your heart, deep within your soul, deep within you.

Every time distrust or lack of trust comes up, watch it, allow it, and find a way to dis-identify from this energy. So you will say, "How do I do this?"

The very process of watching and allowing, without judgment, creates a space in your being, where you can begin to feel detached from the different energies of varied emotions as they move through your body, mind, and heart. This is a choice and a matter of intention and attention.

Cultivating the feeling of knowingness, beyond the doubt and limitations of the mind, requires the practice of dis-identification with unnecessary mind chatter. Suppression and repression of thoughts and judgments will not help. This will make matters worse. Awareness, allowance, and acceptance of what is, are the keys. As I keep repeating, all spiritual practice (meditation, prayer, chanting, *Jappa*) helps to purify and still the mind. The above practices, together with *Yagna* and sacred ceremony to praise the five sacred elements, take you easily and effortlessly into the space within you, which is beyond doubt, which knows, and which is ever flowing and infinitely abundant. Many of you, my darling devotees, have noticed that after a powerful *Aarti* or *Yagna*, you may suddenly feel very full, as though you have eaten a large feast and feelings of bliss and peace emanate from your fields without effort or struggle.

Thank you, Babaji. Spiritual practice is so important in these "End Times" where you can catch a negative thought virus from just walking the streets or watching television, or even looking at advertisements on the underground or subway.

Babaji: For those of you that are choosing the path of truth, love, and simplicity, here now, it is an ongoing challenge for you not to get pulled into the collective doubting that exists amongst a large part of the population with whom you interact on a day-to-day basis. This is when spiritual purification becomes extremely important. If you have spent all day with a crowd of people, where the spiritual IQ is low, and without being a pompous peacock and with genuine humility, you will still need to find ways to effortlessly clear your energy fields of negative vibrations, just like brushing teeth twice a day.

Rashmi practices grounding and protection as a natural part of her beingness and teaches this to her students. My beloved Leonard Orr has spent forty years tirelessly teaching aspirants of the spiritual purification *sadhana* on the *Shiva* path. This purification has also been practiced on other spiritual paths such as by the Essenes, the Sufis, and the Krishna *Bhaktas* (devotees).

Purification with water, through regular bathing; with air, through *pranayama*; purification with fire through *Yagna*, *Aarti* and any other forms of fire cleansing in safety; and spending time in nature is recommended, within balance and as per your inner guidance and common sense.

Purification with the sacred element of earth through fasting from time to time, bathing with salt, working consciously with growing flowers and plants, burning incense leaves, and regular Ayurvedic massage and mud baths, when guided, all help to cleanse and clear your energy and put you in a state of inner silence, purity, and equipoise.

Let it be known that superiority and feeling better than others as a result of purification practices will only incur the displeasure of Lord Shiva. Balance is a key. Cleanliness is next to godliness, and there is no point in saying one is spiritual while not keeping the temple of one's body, mind, heart, and physical home as clean as possible, without being a cleaning fanatic. Integrity of thought, word, and deed is part of spiritual purification, and the *"Om Namah Shivaya" Jappa* is a very powerful way to purify the mind, as I keep repeating.

There are times when the outer is not important, when you can be in the high space without the need for purification, but in general, regular maintenance of your energy bodies and the reverence for the sacred elements, within and without, help you to flower into *samadhi* with greater ease and grace. If you use your spiritual practice as a weapon on a power trip in regards to your fellow brothers and sisters, then your endeavors move from the vibrations of holy nectar to becoming poisonous.

Remember, that if you truly wish to influence others and your environment with the positive vibrations of a balanced spiritual body that is grounded in the here and now, the best way is through being this purity as opposed to preaching it.

Once again any judgment around these issues is to be watched, in order that you may transcend its negative energies. Meanwhile it is important to practice discernment to protect the fragile flower of your spiritual temples of mind, body, and spirit as guided from within yourself.

Each time your inner knowingness and trust are influenced by your own mind, with the energy of doubt and fear, choose trust. And keep choosing it. Remember that energy becomes what it thinks about, as my dear Makhan Singh (Leonard Orr) and Rashmi love to teach. So if you choose trust, you become trust. If you think fear and distrust, you harvest the fruits of fear and a lack of faith. The key is awareness. Another key is watching your mind so that you allow yourself to become aware of the inner dialogues and thereby choose from a place of centered awareness as opposed to unconscious, reactive, habitual, and conditioned or collectively influenced negative patterns. Keep it simple. In simplicity there is great trust. Complexity breeds fear and faithlessness.

If you meditate on a daily basis, trust is a wondrous gift that comes to you naturally. This is because distrust is one of the chief aspects of the continuous rambling of your mind, and meditation brings the detached witnessing of the processes and appetites of your habitual thinking. Let it be known, here, that a purified mind, one that has become well balanced in its marriage with the energies of the heart, is capable of powerful, creative genius that can greatly accelerate human evolution to a place of wise unity and peaceful, harmonious co-creation.

When you sit with fire, it burns off negative karma, apathy, fear and distrust; and in their place you will feel creativity, passion, compassion and peace. If you are in a continuous state of being the detached sashi of your mind, body and intellect, then you will release distrust which requires constant mind chatter. You will also release conditioning and an over attachment to the past and future, where many weeds of distrust are embedded.

Lastly on the subject of trust, your greatest teachers are your children; they can teach you many amazing lessons on trust and play in the here and now. Spend time with them in love and gratitude. If you ask me, I will always help you—though how and when is not something it behooves you to try and control.

OM SHANTI SHANTI SHANTI

OM NAMAH SHIVAYA

Chapter Twelve

TRUTH

There is no question of practicing the virtue of truth and embodying its vibrations without being ready to be courageous, without being prepared, at all times, to think your own thoughts and be your own person.

Babaji: Truth is in silence. Ultimate truth is beyond definition. Within supreme truth are many levels and layers of relative truth. Truth is not a weapon of judgment to use against others. When used in this way, instant karma will be triggered in these current moments of now.

Truth does not require numbers for its validation. Its energy is so total and potent that even a single person fully living and being their truth or supreme truth in the moment can stand up to the opposition of the entire human race.

There are not many of you in my truth army on Earth here now.

I have just a few of you that are at a level of integrity where your thought, word and deed match up and are in harmony with each other. Yet the few will help me to create a blaze of honesty and supreme oneness on this planet in the days to come, into the time beyond time. As I have said before: "You and I are one."

Supreme truth is simple and is generally found in intense silence. This is a powerful silence and a vibration similar to the energy which Rashmiji and many of you have experienced in Haidakhan—my ashram in the foothills of the Himalayas.

Currently, I have my channeler in such a deep space of nothingness, of no-mindedness, and of blue *Chiti Shakti* light, that she is barely able to speak the words of this channeling transmission here now. Rashmi has the feeling that her celestial transcriber, Amravati, is at the other end of a very long blue tunnel of silence and meditative bliss.

I request you the reader to take a moment now away from this book, to close your eyes and to allow yourself to feel this inner world of silent bliss and void.

In this space is the true home of supreme truth. This is why great beings when they finally attain enlightenment (or *Maha Samadi* as I say) on their paths come to a place of total silence and stillness.

There is no question of practicing the virtue of truth and embodying its vibrations without being ready to be courageous, without being prepared, at all times, to think your own thoughts and be your own person.

If you decide to be dishonest, and then remember that ultimately the only one you are really cheating is yourself.

I observe that many of my devotees and people on other spiritual paths are often totally influenced by the opinion of others and the outer authorities of governments, parents, peers and so on. A true aspirant on the path practices moment-to-moment detachment from the good opinion of others or trying to please others. As the wondrous Osho states, a sincere spiritual warrior is essentially a rebel. By this he means, not one that creates anarchy for its own sake, but who is as free as the wind to follow the path of inner wisdom, freedom and truth at the cost of not fitting in with others, with society and the many constraints of day-to-day living.

Tremendous courage is required on the path. The courage to say yes to the truth as it feels right in the moment, and the courage to say no and walk away when the energies are in total conflict with your inner equilibrium, harmony and integrity. Judgment on all of the above will only impede you and create a further mess.

It is a question of delicate balance, great sensitivity and moment-to-moment awareness.

If you lean on the borrowed staff of others for any length of time, you will lose balance and ultimately you will probably have to compromise your integrity and your own inner truth. This does not mean that you must reject the support of others from time to time; just find the balance.

Divine Balance, Divine Balance, Divine Balance.

All spiritual practice brings you ultimately to your inner silence which is your deepest Truth.

OM NAMAH SHIVAYA

Chapter Thirteen

SIMPLICITY

Simplicity is seeing the unity in all things beyond diversity. Simplicity is "beingness" as opposed to "doingness." It simply is.

Babaji: I am Bhole Baba. This means I am the simple Father. The nature of the mind is to be complex and to evaluate, analyze, and to judge. The essential nature of the heart is simplicity. Here we are talking of the spiritual heart within you and not human emotions and feelings. Simplicity is most at home within its hub, which is supreme silence. Simplicity is in the here and now. The mind is always in the past or future and never in the here and now, and therefore is never simple. Once the mind becomes simple, it actually moves to a state of no-mind.

Simplicity is seeing the unity in all things beyond diversity.

Simplicity is "beingness" as opposed to "doingness." It simply IS. Simplicity runs on the limitless energy of acceptance. It tends to be very heartfelt.

When you let go of obsolete ideas, people, places, habits, and material possessions, and also feelings, memories, and thoughts that no longer serve you; you create an emptiness, a space within your being for something new to be born, to be created. There is a new energy that arises within you and this energy is intrinsically simple. You become light, you become silent, all complexity begins to dissolve; restlessness comes to peace, questions no longer arise, and judgment becomes a frequency of the past.

Nature brings you to simplicity immediately and joyfully. Even when you are weathering a dramatic storm, you become essentially simple to be extremely present in the moment in order to survive the fiery elements.

Choosing conscious attention to your conscious intentions brings you to the magic of this wondrous virtue. As I have said before, simplicity always leads you to a place of stillness, silence and peace—even at those times when your personality self may be busy, noisy and in motion. Following the voice of your higher self will lead to simplicity.

I hear you asking the question dear ones:

How do we come to simplicity, while diverse questions, situations, commitments, conflicting agendas bombard us, moment to moment, oftentimes sending us into a tailspin of panic and overwhelm? How do we choose in that moment and what do we choose, and how can we keep it simple when we are creating many different dramas at the same time on the stage of our lives?

When the center is at peace, as I have just said, the periphery can keep spinning at the speed of light. When your center is lost, chaos ensues and you go into a tailspin. Therefore, connecting the root of your being to its home in the center of your inner silence will keep you in balance as things oscillate madly on the circumference of your beingness. Make sure that the roots of the tree of your being are grounded and go deep into the earth of your inner consciousness. This will allow the branches of your personality self to happily cocreate in many different directions, up toward the sky or down toward the earth, without you losing your balance.

The inner core is essentially simple. Unmanifest reality, from which the manifest world springs forth, is essentially pure simplicity in its essence.

Emptiness is simple. A fullness that is born from the bedrock of emptiness may also be simple. A fullness born of complexity and the mental cacophony can never be simple.

Judgment is not simple.

Dishonesty is not simple.

Calculation is not simple (that is over-calculation or when it is out of balance).

Over-analysis is not simple, nor is prejudice.

Apathy may seem to be simple, but it is not so.

Hatred and war are not simple and nor is competition.

If you choose some of the inharmonious energies mentioned above, then you will never know true, lasting, serenity, peace, and silence—enduring simplicity. Children are essentially simple by nature, but unfortunately become complicated when subjected to the conditioning of the overly intellectual and linear thinking of their environment. Silence will always take you to simplicity. Practice it. Practice the inner silence that is strong within you even as you sing, speak, and dance on the stage of your life.

A total involvement in any form of *Karma Yoga*, which takes you beyond your mind to a place of stillness, gives you deep simplicity: such as painting with full absorption, dancing with total passion, and so on. This is meditation in action. Being wholehearted, no matter how passionate, is perfect simplicity.

When you chant OM, you connect strongly to the primordial sound and energy of the universe and to the magical virtues of innocence and "ISNESS," and dis-identify with chaos and confusion, noise and conflict. Keep it simple dear ones!

OM NAMAH SHIVAYA

Chapter Fourteen

BRIDGING OF THE SPIRITUAL
AND THE MUNDANE

*I can assure you, dear ones, that the second phase of my
work—moving humanity to Satya Yuga frequency—is
occurring as we speak and shall be soon completed. You
get to choose heaven by your frequency, or a realm of
limitation, control, greed, manipulation, competition,
and attachment.*

Babaji: I have asked you time and again over the eons, as I have
appeared to you in different bodies which I materialized so as to be
with you.

I have asked you to sacrifice whatever is necessary or what you
are guided to release, moment to moment, to your inner divinity.

There is a time to flow with the incoming tide and a time to ebb.
There is a season for giving and a season for receiving. Unless you
keep emptying that which no longer serves you, one cannot receive
a higher vibration of energy and increase your light and love quotient
which are intrinsic parts of your deepest inner nature.

We, the Ascended Masters, note that humanity's clinging is one of the major causes of your ongoing suffering and dismay.

You can enjoy the many gifts that the divine within you unfolds in your life, and yet to get overly attached to any single object, place, person, preference, prejudice, pain, or pleasure will leave you feeling like you're in a nightmare.

In the times to come, it will be more and more essential for you to tune in to your higher self, the voice of the Divine Mother and Father energies within you, moment to moment. Being in constant balance is now required of you, as you bridge dimensions and move into new vistas of expanded consciousness, where the frequencies of greed, limitation, control, manipulation, and the misuse of power will not be tolerated on any level.

In the near future, all of you who continue to stubbornly cling to the material world and to a limited and selfish outlook will be taken from this realm of reality to a place where the dark *Kali Yuga* energy will be allowed to run its course.

It is not for you to decide whether your friends and family members are essentially moving into the same place in consciousness as yourself. You may, for example, choose to go to the light and they may choose the darkness, or vice versa. They may not be ready to give up third-dimensional reality as they know it on Earth here now. All of you have free will and must make a conscious choice. Each of you has your own unique rhythm and timing.

How exactly all this shall come to pass is not a foregone conclusion; and yet I can assure you, dear ones, that the second phase of my work—moving humanity to *Satya Yuga* frequency—is occurring as we speak and shall be soon completed . You get to choose heaven by your frequency, or a realm of limitation, control, greed, manipulation, competition, and attachment. Which will you choose?

This is what I referred to in the 1980s as the time of *Mahakranti*, or the galvanization of the light and a receding or in many cases, a destruction of all that is dark, dense, and opposing the Unity of All That Is.

I inspire you and encourage you to flow with the frequencies of love, light, and unity that are becoming stronger and stronger in your current human reality, and in opposition to the clinging by some to separation and greed—as these energies are now receding and will soon become history in this realm.

Babaji, we your devotees of old are used to you speaking in this absolute, spiritual warrior, Lord Shiva fashion. However, for those souls that are just beginning to reawaken and reconnect to your energies, what you have just said is extremely frightening. Yet we know that the truth is the truth is the truth and shall stand its ground whether people agree or disagree.

However, it is time for us humans to take responsibility for our choices, our thoughts, our words, and our deeds. If we sow seeds of heaven on earth, we shall grow a heavenly Garden of Eden here now. If we continue to stubbornly sow the seeds of separation and control, then we shall cultivate an arena of hell-like dramas and reality on Earth.

Babaji, money and trust in its flow seem to be even more of an issue as we move toward the light and the dawning of the new age of light and love. It almost feels like an epidemic of control and materialism is on the increase rather than decrease and won't give way to true altruism, philanthropic compassion, and win/win orientation. Of course there are amazing strides in unifying the peoples of this planet and the creation of spiritual communities, organic farming, pollution-free living, and so on. Yet the polarity between this spiritually, intelligent understanding and sheer materialism continue.

Babaji: As you know very well, dear Rashmi, I am the supreme balancing force of the universe and I taught this balancing principle well to my disciples Jesus, Moses, and Elijah. All those that come to me with a sincere heart receive the divine energy of this balancing force within their being. If you are too much into self-sacrifice and can only give to others but not to yourself, I will teach you to receive and receive and receive, so that the energies of giving and taking within you are better integrated. For those that are extremely materialistic and selfish, I might suggest them giving their entire wealth to the divine or some large part of it, for an ashram project as an example, in order to bring divine order into their being.

For those of you that jump straight into the deep end of the spiritual pool without a dollar to your name, I might suggest that when appropriate, you learn to master *Karma Yoga* and play the money game in order to earn a decent living and gain some self-respect.

Remember, dear ones; too much of anything makes the thing ugly. Harmony can only be achieved when there is equilibrium between giving and receiving. While you are in the body on Earth here now, it is important to come to equipoise between functioning in the material world and practicing your spiritual path (sadhana). Going to the extreme of any polarity will lead to a loss of awareness of your center and create chaos and confusion if this stance is maintained in the medium to long term.

Do not take my words too literally! Try to allow your heart to feel the words and more importantly the *Shakti* or energy behind these words.

It is time to give up an obsession with methodology and a compulsive need to know if something is right or something is wrong.

Allow yourself instead to feel your divine dance on earth, here now, to sense and intuit moment-to-moment, spontaneous, effortless, loving flow and kindness to self and others in action and in inaction.

Thank you, Sir Nataraja. Your words cause me to dance within my inner being, where all the atoms and their protons, neutrons, and electrons, and the photons of my light body and its vibrational frequencies are all wondrously dancing, dancing, joyfully and ecstatically irrespective of whether I have ten pounds or ten million in the bank.

So Babaji, with this freak-out that many have experienced individually and collectively on flow in our lives, could you shed a little more light on how to ease the symptoms of the disease of lack?

Babaji: Rashmiji, in all the years since you jumped off the cliff by leaving your homes all over the world and truly embracing your spiritual path here in London's Kensington, you have had many challenges . . . but have you been left lacking for even a split second?

No you have not! Yet you have worried from time to time about whether the flow would suddenly stop, and you would no longer have money to pursue your spiritual path, to help others, and to have money to buy chocolates and take rides in taxis.

I must praise you, dear one, for your immense courage to continually face your fear of being foolhardy with money while following the bidding of the divine voice within you on your path of service to humanity and your addiction to Coca Cola (just kidding).

In recent time I have impulsed you to let go of your flat in London and to be "homeless," to make everywhere you go your home, to jump on airplanes, to write spiritual books, and to make spiritual TV shows and films. I know that at times you have felt that you are about to go crazy at the idea of losing the roof over your head to pay for these incredible spiritual goals!

Yet you face your fear and you never let these fears of lack stop you from following the voice of your Higher Self.

What I am saying here is: of course fear may come up on the path, and in fact it always does, particularly as one is asked to be more and more courageous with the energy of one's soul and the *paramatma* (divine) energy within. If you choose to follow the dictates of your fear, you will stay in states of illusion and delusion which is the essential nature of fear. If you move bravely forward into and through fear and allow love and oneness to be your true boss, then your whole reality begins to open up to being one of harmonious love, harmonious flow, and synchronistic beauty and peace. As is the case for my dear channel, this beloved spiritual beauty.

I know in my heart that if the flow does stop that I will find a new and better way and so will the rest of mankind. But it breaks my heart to see people starving, homeless, and struggling to keep warm and healthy. So I try and help whomever I can as best as possible without going into debt and balancing self-love with the love of others.

Babaji: The karmic playing out of other people's dramas is ultimately not your business. This does not mean being apathetic or using it as an excuse for being dispassionate. I will say this to you my dear human children.

1. Learn to love yourself and be honest about this process.

2. From reaping the wealth of spiritual practice, allow the overflow of this abundance to be shared with others in a way that is innocent and detached.

3. Practice the wisdom of the inner, intuitive, feeling body on when to give and when to say no.

In the time to come, dear ones, you will move away from money as you know it, food as you know it, and sex and procreation as you know them. There will be a new pattern and a new order based 100 percent on truth, love, and simplicity. You will become pure light, which you are now but have forgotten. You will be able to anchor this light in some sort of body form that is a lot less dense than what you experience here now, and yet you will be able to also watch yourself participating in various levels of consciousness—dimensions as you say—at the same time and also beyond time. There will come a time when you will not require food to sustain yourself which most of you require here now. And procreation will be transformed as well. Many of these changes are beyond your wildest imaginings and definitely beyond the comprehension of your mind.

They are however not beyond the feelings of your heart and the wisdom of your deep innate knowingness which is within you.

You and I are One.

When you are happy I am happy.

When you are sad I am sad.

Be a dynamo of irrepressible joy.

Love all, serve all.

Praise every soul.

If you cannot praise someone, allow them to pass out of your life and by that I don't mean by giving them a shove. Do so as gently, as neutrally and with as much detachment and genuineness as possible.

Ask and you shall receive no matter how you block receiving, even when you doubt and when you do not trust your knowingness that you will receive. In fact, there is no will about it. Know that you are receiving here and now. How much are you willing to accept?

How deserving are you feeling of this great flow?

How unlimited are you going to allow yourself to be in becoming great gods/goddesses in the making?

The more you believe in lack, the more you focus on it, the more you fear it, the more you suppress it and the more you resist it, the greater will be the energy of lack in your life.

Allow flow, empty yourself to receive, give/take, hold and let go, rest and work, work and rest; be like a rose silent and yet serving through its beauty and fragrance for all.

Shri Laxmi Namah
Shri Ganesha Namah
Jai Maha Maya Ki Jai
Om

OM NAMAH SHIVAYA

Chapter Fifteen

DARE TO BE YOUR TRUTH

I wish for you to seek harmony at all times, but not at the cost of the truth . . . to become spiritual warriors and take up the sword of light to cut through the darkness, cut through illusion and delusion, and to fight the good fight— the fight for integrity, unity, love, for peace and most of all for the integral truth.

Babaji: I am the manifestation of heaven and earth here now. I contain within me the Divine Mother and the Divine Father energies. I contain the male and the female energies of the universe and yet I am beyond sexual gender. I am the supreme teaching principle of divine being and becoming. Ultimately there is no "I" and therefore that which be "me" is a phenomena of *Maha Avataric* energy, which is beyond definition and beyond comprehension of the ego self.

From the eyes of your heart, in moments of deep sincerity and when you receive my grace and benediction, you may have intense or subtle glimpses of the vast expansive energy of love, light, sound, and the divine which I represent. The more you try to fathom me through your intellect, the further I recede from your reality. If you will allow yourself to become like a little child and open yourself up in innocence and with sincere heartfelt devotion, I will fill you with harmony and love and truth and simplicity.

Continuously chasing after pleasure and a perpetual resistance to and running away from pain is the nature of the mind. Your desire for pleasure is endless and so is your resistance to pain and suffering.

I am asking you now to choose from a higher order, a more exalted wholeness, where you choose from the energy of your soul, from the fragrance of your deepest inner sacred heart.

I wish for you to choose unity from within and beyond diversity, to select the bridging of many different flavors and opposing energies. Choose *Ananda* and let go of your obsession with pleasure. *Ananda*, or true bliss and ecstasy, arises from the bedrock of *Atma* and *Paramatma*. *Ananda* is therefore eternal and real. Pleasure rises and falls from the waves of *Maya* that are weaved through the mind with its endless desires. The fulfillment of these desires is therefore always ephemeral, and if pleasure is to be experienced in its ultimate totality, it moves to pain—deep unbearable agony. This pleasure arises from the ego self, which is ultimately illusionary and fickle in its orientation.

I want you to be brave. I wish for you to choose wisely now and to pierce through the veils of *Maya* to rediscover your home in the silence, the oneness, the organic wholeness and completeness that exists quite naturally as your true, intrinsic, deep, inner nature—your *Tat Tvam Asi* (I Am That Presence).

I wish for you to seek harmony at all times, but not at the cost of the truth. I wish for you now to become spiritual warriors and take up the sword of light to cut through the darkness, cut through illusion and delusion, and to fight the good fight within you—the fight for integrity, unity, love, for peace and most of all for the integral truth, moment to moment. I wish for you to be humble in a real way and not just masquerade humility. At the same time I ask you to be centered in the power of your truth, the power of your love, and the power of your daring.

I would like you to dare, dare, and dare some more.

Come out of your little boxes of what you think is your reality and what you think is possible, and to keep pushing those boundaries to new frontiers of being and becoming.

Keep checking yourself, dear ones; do not blindly follow authority figures such as politicians, pop stars, and so-called spiritual and religious leaders without testing the integrity of the spiritual waters in which they swim. I note that many of you particularly in the so-called new age movement in the West and also in the East are making a pretentious claim to truth, love, and simplicity. If you own a great deal of wealth and are not clinging to it on the deepest levels, you are still a lot simpler than someone who may appear to be simple and/or poor but is clinging to ideology and possessions in a very tenacious sort of way. If you choose to misunderstand me now, this will only cause you more pain.

To be a true spiritual Babaji warrior requires you to be ready to give up anything I ask of you, at a moment's notice. My Bholi, Rashmiji, has been asked to sleep on a very thin mattress for weeks by the fire in my Len Raja's training centre, answering endless questions over several weeks on metaphysical subjects and about me as well. As a spiritual princess, she did this well and went to zero, even though it was extremely uncomfortable for her. Mind you she loves fire. Straight after this, I requested that she spent months in a chic hotel called the Omni to do morphogenic work for the healing of America and its peoples. She has followed my guidance in spite of huge expenses and a complete lack of logic as she has watched her bank balance quickly diminish. Leonard Orr and Sondra Ray have served me tirelessly for the last thirty to forty years at great personal sacrifice. Many of you—and you know who you are—have served me and have received the grace and benediction of those who bravely and wholeheartedly serve the divine. Amravati and Rashmi have been meeting over the past several weeks for the purposes of the channeling and transcription of this book, in spite of great challenges, distractions, and intense initiation in their personal lives.

Babaji, you are so beautiful. You are truly Satyam Shivam Sundaram. You are my first, my last, my everything. I have journeyed through many, many lifetimes with you through the eons. I have been serving you single-pointedly in the last fifteen years of linear time, but our connection goes back through time and space to the realm of the unmanifest bliss and effulgence.

As I have mentioned, I am very happy to follow thy bidding, even when it may not be logical, convenient, and require great personal sacrifice and detachment. I do not see all this work of coming to zero—sometimes financially, emotionally, and physically—as suffering.

We have to take responsibility for choosing to walk hand in hand with the divine. I may joke and complain about Babaji making me do something, but in my deepest heart I know that you don't "make" me do anything. You guide me and either I choose to follow the voice of my higher self, which is you within me, or I choose to spiral into the unconscious agendas of my limited ego self. I choose vis-a-vis my heart and soul as they know that I am here on earth to serve the divine plan and to wake up now to the limitless aspect of who I be and also help others along the way. As one becomes spiritually wiser, one begins to have a deep awareness that there is no separation between the Soul and the Oversoul. I know that you and I, Babaji, are one. Yet, I miss the times when you appeared to me in wonderful transcendental states, but the fact is that my current experience of our oneness is far closer to the truth of the flowering of my self-realization.

People have to let go of this obsession with, "Is this right or is this wrong?" The wise practice of spirituality requires the seeker to consciously choose from a space of heart-centeredness and to take responsibility for the repercussions of that choice.

Babaji: Correct. This confusion over choosing to serve the divine one minute and bewailing how tormented one is by being bossed around by the divine the next is not integrity! It is extreme futility! If you choose the truth and the way of love and the way of the sacred, you will slowly and surely have to let go of greed, dishonesty, competition, and selfishness. You cannot take these dark energies with you if you are to weed out all that is false in your life.

Thank you, Babaji. It is a great challenge for me here now to see my family going in one direction while my path continues strongly on its journey to the "within." It is very hard when one's loved ones condemn and criticize your deepest inner knowingness and spiritual flowering just because it is the opposite of living in a very linear, materialistic way for its own sake. With your grace and through self-healing, I have been able to come to a place where the opinion of others matters less and less. My students—and human beings in general—find this very difficult: being detached and not needing the assurance and reassurance and appreciation of others. (Since writing this my family has magically had a deeper understanding of my path.)

Some of us are working continuously behind the scenes where applause or thank-you's is out of the question, and oftentimes so is being paid for the work. When we begin to see the bigger picture, we realize that none of this matters and the divine being that we are is far greater than issues of profit and loss and of condemnation and adulation.

Babaji: Even now, in spite of the energies of light cascading in this realm, very few of you understand what you have just explained, Rashmi, in the deepest part of your inner knowing and right action. I wish for you, my devotees, to come away from the adulation of popular outer authority and a hankering for name and fame for its own sake. Do what needs to be done, say what needs to be said, go where you are asked to be by your divine nature. Keep it simple.

If you come together in *satsang*, do so not to be superior to others but to exalt the divinity within yourself and to celebrate the divinity within each other. It pains me when many of you come together in *satsang* in my name and practice elitism and separation and have a stance of superiority. This is not what I have come to teach you. If this is what you are practicing, forgive yourself and choose differently in the new moment of now. Coming to Haidakhan is an extremely holy pilgrimage; and yes it does resolve karma and it does bring deep grace to your life, yet it does not absolve you from the simple practice of truth, simplicity, and love in your life, moment to moment.

I am here to destroy all the negative poisons of your egocentric ways. I am here to exalt the light, love, and sacred sound that you be, within your free will.

Find the right distance from me, moment to moment. If you come too close to me too soon in an unintegrated way, you shall burn up. If you stay too far away, then the light and fire of my love will not reach you, will not warm you, and will be unable to illuminate you.

Babaji, could you illuminate us on the subject of projection.

Babaji: Blame and shame are a loser's game.
Projecting on another in the name of fame
leads not to the birth of a pristine spiritual dame
Ignite within integrity's eternal flame.

Do you like this ditty?

Very much.

Babaji: Blaming others, your governments, your parents, and so on does not serve you. This form of behavior will keep you in a dense, dark, confused, and egocentric consciousness. Come out of the quicksand of projecting onto others your own painful, misjudged, unacceptable, or denied parts of being. It is important to be quiet and to make space for silence, to have an intimate relationship with oneself: one's motivations, one's desires and one's shadow side. If you don't spend time alone, how will you know who you are or what you are denying within yourself? If you can't find the time and space for this form of self-love, you will never be able to love another for you have not learned how to love yourself.

Ultimately it is important for you to embrace even the dark parts of your being that you judge to be wrong or bad or undesirable. Hand over your guilt, your fear, your self-hatred, your resistance to the Divine Mother and Father energies for alchemical transmutation. If you bathe in fire—and I don't mean jump into it; I mean bathe in the aura of firelight—the fire acts as a giant celestial Hoover and vacuums out a lot of negative thinking, undesirable karma, and brings you back to the truth, simplicity, and love that is your intrinsic nature (beneath the dust of ignorance).

Seek further transmutation in nature. As I keep saying, dear ones, nature is a master healer. Nature is the divine in physical form. Nature is pure and innocent. It is the energy of pure beingness, and while birth, growth, preservation, death, and decay occur within Mother Nature's breast, she is essentially the energy of pure beingness.

She can heal you from the worst effects of your self-importance, your extreme fatigue from over-doingness, and the constant chatter of your monkey mind. Practice deep breathing in nature. Become one with Mother Nature, and remember when I create great storms and havoc in your lives, these are but divine *leelas* which help to remove the cobwebs of ignorance, lethargy, stubbornness, and being persistently stuck. So laugh with the howl of the wind in the storm, and dance with the blizzard and snowflakes and feel my love clearing you, healing, and taking you to a new place: a pristine, clean self at the end of the thunder and the lightning.

However, this will take patience. And I will infuse you with the energy of patience and tolerance, without compromising your integrity if you but ask. I wish you all now to become patience, especially you Rashmiji, and yes I know your name is Rashmi. Without patience you are constantly subjected to the negative energies or faulty understanding of authority or influences outside of yourself.

Babaji, my dear friend Penelope channeled that it behooves me to step back into Self on a regular basis before stepping forward again to perform multiple tasks on my spiritual path, such as channeling spiritual books, counseling others, making spiritual films, and conducting individual and global morphogenetic healing. But the most powerful way to step back into oneself is meditating, being in nature, creating something wholeheartedly, or just being still and quiet alone.

I note that most human beings do not allow themselves this simple blissful practice.

I find when I do allow myself this space and time that I come away feeling recharged, rejuvenated, relaxed, released of angst, and ready to charge forward again in love and trust.

I find that when I slow down, I am actually able to achieve more by doing less and it all becomes effortless and easy.

Babaji: Well said. Do not be distracted on the path, and trust that I will complete the holy task of the liberation of this plane.

Envy and jealousy of others depletes your spiritual energy and distracts you from the peace of your inner temple of sacred silence.

As best you can, release all resentment, neutralize anger, and let go of negativity before you do, say, or create anything or otherwise your words, your deeds, and your creation will be contaminated with the energy of darkness, heaviness, and negativity.

Without the cultivation of the blossoms of surrender within your being, there is no question of the unfolding of supreme divinity within you. Surrender to the Divine Mother/Father energies within and without in a spiritually intelligent, alert, moment-to-moment way.

I wish for you to live in a state of perpetual peace and harmony, but I would like to make it clear that this harmonious state should never be achieved through the lack of courage and at the cost of truth and integrity.

OM NAMAH SHIVAYA

Chapter Sixteen

GRACE AND PURITY OF HEART

I wish for you to be ordinary in your extraordinariness and make it okay to be extraordinary within the simple, peaceful ordinariness of your being. As I keep saying, don't take things too literally, come out of the mind and feel the energy of my teaching in your heart, which is beyond words.

Babaji: Let it be known that, no matter how deeply you master the wisdom of Cosmic Consciousness on the path toward enlightenment, this is ultimately not the greatest supreme truth; it is the truth of divine consciousness. By this I mean that all things are subject to impurity once they move out of the unmanifest realm into being manifest reality. Many of you have asked yourselves and each other as to how, even though I am *Maha Avatar*, I was still subject to disease and early death of my 1970/80's body as Haidakhan Baba. Many of the greatest saints and enlightened beings on earth have passed over through diseases like heart attacks and cancer, and I was no exception.

This is because, as I have just clarified to you, even the divine *Avataric* energy, when stepped down into the physical realm in a physical body, is to a certain extent subject to the laws of 3rd dimensionality, the laws of the relative.

I wish for you now, my beloved children, to aim for the highest spiritual attainment, which is beyond a deep esoteric understanding of cosmic consciousness (though it contains this knowledge and experiential wisdom). Intend to become one with the divine truth, which has its home in the unmanifest, in supreme silence, in the great void, and in divine mystery and can be accessed in deep meditation, transcendental states, and mystical experience. Ask for the grace of these celestial boons. This illumination and wisdom cannot be commanded and demanded but can be achieved through grace, prayer, wholehearted devotion to the divine, and wholehearted service to all everywhere. Keep moving on the spiritual path from the lower truth to higher truth, until you come to that place deep within you, one that is silent, that is peaceful, and that is pure beingness and beyond judgment. As you progress, keep letting go of the many impurities that get stuck to the so-called religious and spiritual paths and "isms." For example, if you are preaching compassion while being selfish and unaware of your own energy and where it is stuck in impurity, then you are deluding yourself that you are a compassionate person.

It is important for my people to "walk their talk." As I keep telling you, impeccability of thought, word, and deed will bring great grace into your life right now. To follow half-baked spiritual leaders and mediocrity will no longer serve you and will only increase your suffering.

I require for you to be wholehearted. Half-heartedness falls short. When you are half-hearted about something, you create half a space in your being for ignorance and negativity to come through into your being and latch on to you. Remember when you fool yourself, this leads to the greatest misery of all. There is no point in continuing to be a hypocrite. There is no point in talking about peace and having thoughts of war, hate, and distrust. If you say that you are openminded and openhearted, make sure that you begin to match these energies in thought, word, and deed.

Once you become simple and release the shadow through recognizing it, releasing judgment and forgiving yourself, you become the light, you become peace, and you are supreme silence. This allows great energy, synchronicity, and flow to enter and a letting go or a falling away of struggle, blame, shame, and victimhood. Weed your garden of all dishonesty within yourself—be it mental, physical, emotional, or spiritual.

The time of Kali is here now. The goddess Kali will destroy all dishonesty, mental filth, prejudice, insincerity, and greed. If you are compromised by the darkness, you have a very good chance of catching the disease of ignorance and of totally dimming the light of the spiritual knowingness within you. Why choose the depths of such a hell of negative consciousness and darkness when peace, love, truth, and simplicity are your intrinsic inner nature and are flourishing in the Age of Aquarius—the time to wake up to the Satya Yuga frequencies.

It is time now to let go of your identification with your name, your nationality, and all the other assorted labels that have been given to you from outside sources. You are a cosmic being and becoming and ultimately you are pristine, divine, silent, omniscient, pure potentiality—the unmanifest.

But, also remember, dear ones: the siddhis (magical abilities) are not granted by the divine to those who will misuse power and act solely and wholly from the agenda of the ego-oriented psyche. The divine will take away these celestial gifts when a particular entity moves from unity consciousness and love to delusions of grandeur, separateness, and control. I wish for you to be ordinary in your extraordinariness and make it okay to be extraordinary within the simple, peaceful ordinariness of your being. As I keep saying, don't take things too literally, come out of the mind and feel the energy of my teaching in your heart which is beyond words.

Ask for the grace to be helped where you are stuck.

As you know dear ones, Universal law is paradoxical and therefore quite humorous. Yes, you as humanity are in a totally free-will zone where the Creator allows you to choose, and the law of cause and effect give you the fruits of those choices. As I have said before, it is time for you to take total responsibility for the choices you make consciously and subconsciously and to stop pointing the finger. The paradox, of the law of free will on earth, is the law that to totally become one with divine truth within and without, one is eventually required to totally surrender the will of one's ego to the divine will within.

Ultimately, the divine plan and the plan of your divine self within—let's call it your soul's agenda—are one. The ego usually has a very different scheme. True Divinity can only be accomplished through surrendering to the divine within and without as I have just said. Basically the energy of divine will is far greater than the energy of the will of the ego. You know this intellectually and yet you do not follow this wisdom. It is okay to allow your personality/ego self its unique flavor and its individual stance as long as at the core, the divine will is your equalizer, overriding influence on all levels at all times.

This helps to purify the ego self and helps it to move away from separation, limitation, and control toward a wondrous flowering of an unique individuality arising from within the innate wisdom of the oneness, the organic wholeness, and the non-separation of all people, places, ideas, and energies.

I wish for you as warriors of awareness to be alert, to be aware, to be ready and to be totally flexible moment to moment. The new world is at your doorstep. Prepare for the dawning of an age of great love, light, and unity.

Babaji, thank you from the bottom of our hearts for being with us so strongly and powerfully here now, and sharing with us your vision for a new world from the vast ocean of your unfathomable wisdom and love. We are truly, truly in deep awe and gratitude for this celestial transmission that we have received in the past few weeks. I will endeavor with as much courage, energy, and spiritual power as I can muster, and with your grace, to make these wisdom teachings available to people all over the world who are seeking to bridge the old with the new. These wisdom teachings will facilitate the bridging of diversity and the finding of peaceful harmonious ways in order to resolve:

> *the unequal distribution of wealth on this planet,*
> *the deep suffering that arises from ignorance,*
> *the problems of ecological pollution, and*
> *the conflicts that lead to war on Earth.*

There are many that do not believe that war will end on Earth here now, and yet millions are waking up to a higher vibration, a greater sense of trusting in an exponential evolution, the quantum leap to a higher vibration and the paradigm of peace and heaven on earth.

Babaji: My dearest Rashmi and my darling humanity, I love you all dearly as I have said: I am in your every breath. I feel your every pain and all the joy of your hearts, individually and collectively. As you know, I will see you through to your enlightenment from the darkness to the full reinstatement of a consciousness of light, love, and truth.

Keep tuning in to me, and your journey to this new vista of expansive beingness will be joyous, harmonious and full of bliss and mirth.

Those of you who will continue to stubbornly choose survival, competition, struggle, control, separation, and needless suffering will be allowed to play out your dramas of limitation and *Kali Yuga* darkness! You are in a free-will zone.

Let it be known though, that this obsession with the dark will become increasingly difficult to practice as a wave of supreme light consciousness sweeps your third dimensional reality, and transforms it into the eternal newness of the Unified field of Oneness.

No matter how many miracles occur in your life and how many mystical experiences you may enjoy, I want you to remember the silence and the simplicity of who you be. No matter how much spirituality you attain, remember that if you become too egotistical about it, you will lose these states of being and fall from grace.

Total grace demands total purity and simplicity of the heart that sees the oneness in the diversity and serves this oneness steadfastly at all times and on all levels. Only such a one of pristine impeccability will go through the eye of the needle and be able to walk through the cleansing fire and overcome the storms and earth-birth changes of *Mahakranti*. Let us go into the silence now, let us become one in this silence together, let us merge into the ocean of oneness and from this merging, and let us become nothing, nowhere—just pure beingness, supreme bliss, and supreme ecstasy. All is one.

OM NAMAH SHIVAYA

Chapter Seventeen

RASHMI'S CONCLUSION

I don't know about you, but as far as I am concerned, Babaji is truly awesome and while entertaining and completely adorable, let us not forget that he is not ultimately separate from us but the deepest part of our own inner Divine Mother/Father nature.

If we pray with true sincerity and as much love as we can feel authentically in any given moment to the Divine Mother/Father energies of the universe, the Source will always hear our call and respond.

A beautiful fox just appeared in the garden, and though we had to shoo it away in order not to disturb the cats, it was a fabulous reminder from Babaji that the celestial energy of Source can come to us in so many beautiful, wonderful, and oftentimes mysterious ways. If just a few of us truly imbibe and become a part of the light which we already are but have forgotten, Babaji says these few can spread the fire of his light and love everywhere.

This and other sacred books contain the living light energy of the Ascended Ones. When these vibrations touch our lives, we move from being the caterpillar to becoming the interdimensional butterfly. I surrender my heart; I surrender my energy of love, pure intention, and forgiveness of self and others on the path, at the Lotus Feet of my beloved Sadguru within—Maha Avatar Haidakhan Babaji.

Now I will go into meditation and journey to the special cave that Babaji has made for me high up in the Himalayan Mountains to be with him and bask in his sacred fire and be with my baby tiger cub Shakti (another wonderful present from Babaji). As we sit peacefully together in this celestial abode, the sound of OM will permeate through the ethers, and all will be at peace and at one and will cherish being present on earth here now. This is heaven on earth for me.

Om Shanti, Shanti, Shanti, Om

OM NAMAH SHIVAYA

ACKNOWLEDGMENTS

I would like to thank my most beloved Babaji for this incredible spiritual journey and sacred work.

I would also like to thank my awesome earthly team: Robert Friedman, my visionary publisher and friend; John Nelson, my wonderful intuitive editor and friend; Amravati for her dedicated transcribing; and Jonathan Friedman for his superb graphics.

BIOGRAPHY OF RASHMI KHILNANI

 Rashmi Khilnani was born in Chandigarh, Mother India. She has been a channel for the Ascended Masters for the last fifteen years. Her connection to Lord Shiva goes back through eons of lifetimes. Rashmi has always had a great passion for serving Shri Maha Avatar Babaji 1008, the Christ Yogi and Ascended Master who will guide us on the Earth plane until all seven billion plus human beings attain Christ (Unity) Consciousness.

In the last fifteen years, she has studied and taught with world-renowned gurus and teachers and has become a specialist in energy medicine. She is on the forefront of bringing the ancient mystery school teachings of India, Tibet, China, Egypt, and the teachings of the Essenes into the modern era and making them simple and accessible to people of all levels of soul journeying. These sacred wisdom transmissions can assist in day-to-day problem solving in current time.

Rashmi teaches and practices several healing modalities and has taught Reiki Masters, doctors, scientists, and people from many walks of life, the secrets of the Mystery School teachings. She has facilitated the healing and transformation of many thousands through the different streams of "Reiki Energy Mastery" teaching and healing. She is a global metaphysical teacher, author, urban shaman, international lecturer, artist, seminar leader, and TV personality.

Rashmi utilizes her psychic gifts for intuitive channeling, and the application of sound, light, and breathwork for vibrational healing. Through these medium, she helps to shift and heal individuals and groups and conducts ceremonies for morphogenic, global, and heart healing. She seeks to serve the Ascended Masters in bringing a spiritualization and the heartfelt quality of unconditional love and unity consciousness to people of all walks of life. She also works and trains her Reiki Master students in the healing and rebalancing of the Sacred Elements and Mother Earth herself.

At this time, leading up to 2012 and the end time of the Mayan Calendar, the photonic energy is making it possible for many souls across the globe to open up to the pure heartfelt frequencies of unity consciousness and unconditional love.

Rashmi Khilnani is the author of *The Divine Mother Speaks, the Healing of the Human Heart* and *The Buddha Speaks to the Buddha Nature within*. She is currently co-producing a documentary film on God.

Rashmi wishes you, her fellow spiritual brothers and sisters, a deep sense of meditative peace and awareness.

Om Namah Shivaya
Jai Maha Maya Ki Jai
Bhole Baba Ki Jai

To find out more about Rashmi log on to
www.rashmikhilnani.com and
www.reiki-energy-mastery.com

RELATED TITLES

If you enjoyed Shiva Speaks, you may also enjoy other Rainbow Ridge titles. Read more about them at *www.rainbowridgebooks.com*.

The Divine Mother Speaks: The Healing of the Human Heart
by Rashmi Khilnani

The Buddha Speaks: To the Buddha Nature Within by Rashmi Khilnani

The Cosmic Internet: Explanations from the Other Side by Frank DeMarco

Conversations with Jesus: An Intimate Journey by Alexis Eldridge

Dialogue with the Devil: Enlightenment for the Unwilling by Yves Patak

Dance of the Electric Hummingbird by Patricia Walker

Coming Full Circle: Ancient Teachings for a Modern World by Lynn Andrews

*Afterlife Conversations with Hemingway: A Dialogue on
His Life, His Work and the Myth* by Frank DeMarco

*Consciousness: Bridging the Gap Between Conventional Science
and the New Super Science of Quantum Mechanics* by Eva Herr

Jesusgate: A History of Concealment Unraveled by Ernie Bringas

Messiah's Handbook: Reminders for the Advanced Soul by Richard Bach

Blue Sky, White Clouds by Eliezer Sobel

Rainbow Ridge Books publishes spiritual and metaphysical titles,
and is distributed by Square One Publishers in Garden City Park, New York.
To contact authors and editors, peruse our titles, and see submission guide-
lines, please visit our website at *www.rainbowridgebooks.com*.
For orders and catalogs, please call toll-free: (877) 900-BOOK.